NEITHER SLAVE NOR FREE

Helping Women Answer the Call to Church Leadership

Patricia Gundry

1817

Harper & Row, Publishers, San Francisco

Cambridge, Hagerstown, New York, Philadelphia, Washington
London, Mexico City, São Paulo, Singapore, Sydney

FIRST EDITION

Library of Congress Cataloging-in-Publication Data

Gundry, Patricia.
  Neither slave nor free.

  Bibliography: p.
  1. Women in Christianity.   I. Title.
BV639.W7G86   1987   262'.0088042   86–45808
ISBN 0–06–063529–0

87 88 89 90 91 HC 10 9 8 7 6 5 4 3 2 1

Contents

Foreword

It seems to me that an inevitable item on our agenda is to ask ourselves what are we doing? What do we want? And how is the best way to get it?

When we first ask these questions, we get answers like: We are working to be accepted as fully participating members of our churches. We want full acceptance of our equal humanity. And we will do it the way we have seen men do this sort of thing.

Eventually someone like me muses out loud, "What if we asked ourselves these questions again after first asking ourselves, 'Who are we?' " When I ask myself those questions again after asking and answering "Who are we?" I get different answers. Who are we? We are believers, Christ ones, Christians. We are the Church as fully and completely as any person of any gender ever has been or ever will be. We are the Church? Yes, *we are* the Church.

That changes every answer. For if we are the church we do not need to be allowed into the structures of privilege and power. We do not have to minister in the accepted way within those structures. When I share this realization with other women their eyes widen with surprise and then recognition. They begin to think about it. Later, when I see them again, they say things like "I've been discovering implications all over the place since you said that. I can hardly wait to put my new ideas into practice."

If we are the church we do not need permission to minister. You must know that ordination, that sought after and longed for credentialing, is a totally human invention. It isn't a biblical requirement for ministry, it isn't a practical requirement for ministry, it isn't even a historical requirement for ministry. Dwight L. Moody was certainly a person with a ministry, and he was never ordained and never sought ordination. He purposefully avoided it.

If we are the Church we can minister as the Spirit and our spirit and inclinations lead us, one by one as individuals, and cooperatively in groups. We have the needs *and* the gifts among us to minister to our needs ourselves. We can minister to whomsoever will come and receive, female or male.

MOVING OUTSIDE FORM TO LOOK AT FUNCTION

We have all too easily beaten ourselves bloody knocking at the closed doors of the institutional Church asking to be allowed into the established avenues of ministry, thinking all the while that this is the way to do it. Well, it is one way, not a very good way, perhaps, and certainly not the only way.

Actually, if we think about it, many of us will admit that we always thought some of those avenues were too stylized and rigid and outdated anyway. We really would like in to improve things, to innovate some, refurbish the place a bit.

Why keep knocking to get in? Why not circumvent the obstacles entirely and re-invent the Church along more vital, even more biblical lines? A lot of deadwood has accumulated over the centuries. Quite a few antique structures have lost their functional effectiveness. Why not leave them to a museum and get on with the living organism that is the church?

If we were to do that, just how could we go about it? We could merely step outside the established forms for ministry and look at function. We could ask, "What is needed? What do we have to offer?" Then match need with gifts and inclinations, abilities and talents, imaginations, and leadings of the Holy Spirit. Go directly to the Source.

THE VALUE AND FREEDOM OF ORIGINAL THOUGHT

When people with ability are shut out of an established way of doing things, they tend to generate *new* ways of doing things. And those ways frequently turn out to be better—not because the people generating them are necessarily superior in ability, but because, over time, institutional structures decay. New ways can sidestep red tape and the "can't do things differently because we've always done it this way" mentality.

There is also the underdog vitality factor. It's the, "We try harder because we're Number Two," that a car rental agency made money with for many years. It worked because people recognize that it's true.

But to generate new and better ways of ministry, we need the freedom for individual thought to flourish and surface. We need people who make discoveries and act on them, even if that action is only sharing the information with others who are good at implementing great ideas. Women are becoming able to allow themselves to think and discover, to listen to the Spirit within, and say, "Why not? Why not me? Why not do it?"

When a new idea is put into practice, a new idea for ministry, or a way of thinking about ministry that comes from this freedom of individual thought (which, incidentally, only happens when individual women begin taking themselves and their minds and spiritual value seriously) a change that may have been small begins to generate other changes. No change happens in a vacuum. If you create or innovate a ministry, it will in turn generate other ministries. Others will hear of it and generate ideas of their own. Still others will experience the results and go on to contribute from their own resources, in their own way. So one change begins many. Life proliferates.

1. What's Happening?

It wasn't too long ago that I cried myself to sleep because of an excess accumulation of church-dispensed propaganda on the inferiority of women (oppression in the name of Christ, I call it). I was so devastated that I was beginning to almost believe the Holy Spirit in me was somehow not the same Holy Spirit that indwelled "the brethren," or if otherwise why am I to keep quiet in the church and not let that Holy Spirit speak through me, simply because I have a woman's body? God surely makes more sense than that. But they pointed to Holy Scripture for "proof" and I was about to sink under it. "Bring your pies, ladies, but leave your ideas at home." Our pastor, in addressing a group of young girls, . . . laid it on them that they could never be pastors but they could do other things—like bake a pie for a church supper. If I sound angry, I am, but it just seethes inside me. I don't say much here. This is a small town in rural————, and to challenge the traditions of male dominance here is to rush in where angels fear to tread. But I'm gathering enough strength to question the things they tell me I must believe. "It will come," they tell me, "You'll understand someday." I think at last I'm beginning to!*

This excerpt from a letter poignantly reveals the dilemma in which many women find themselves. Feeling isolated, hurt, fearful, and angry, they want to make changes. But change seems almost impossible. Letters like this one, conversations over the phone and face-to-face with many other women, all with their own stories and situations, but in a way all the same, have made me want to find a way to bring them together. If I could, I would do that, showing them that they are not alone, that many others share their feelings, experiences, and conflicts. Then I would want to make sure they shared resources, profiting from each other's learnings.

I know I cannot literally gather these women together in one large room. But I can do what I *can* do, and that is share what I have discovered through my own experiences and observations, along with the things other women have told me about theirs. This book is here in your hand to do that. It is personal, from me to you. And it is

*Unless otherwise indicated, all quotes opening chapters are from private correspondence.

practical, born of real experience. It's hopeful, because I am an optimistic realist.

Here is how it all began.

WHERE WE WERE

I don't know the year it appeared because back then I didn't realize one must write down where and when and on which page such clippings came from for future use. But I have in my file a photograph, from a national women's magazine, of a church sign (the kind with moveable letters one can announce sermons or events on, or say whatever one pleases). The words are easily read and to the point.

Beneath the name of the church, the times of the services, and the name of the pastor, it says,

ADAMS RIB, PLUS
SATANS FIB EQUALS
WOMANS LIB

That sign succinctly represents the conflict I saw approaching within the Church. I began seriously to think about writing a book that had been simmering on a back burner of my mind for several years.

I had, for a long time, been puzzled by interpretations of various Bible passages regarding women. As a Bible believer, I felt sure there were good and reasonable explanations for seemingly contradictory verses. I had always thought that *someday* I would research it all and write about it. But I wanted to wait until I had more writing experience. Not only did I feel inadequate to the task, but I hoped also that later I would be well-enough known to ensure a wide reading audience for what I knew would be a very important subject.

But the issue was building because of activities in the secular world among newly awakened feminists. Churches were doing outrageous things, like putting up signs on their marquees that were insulting to women and foolhardy in their blanket condemnation of women working for equal opportunities in our society.

I looked for something written on the subject from a biblical perspective. But I could find nothing for the woman in the pew, and very little for anyone else. I decided that the book needed to be born even if I felt unready for the birth. And so I wrote *Woman Be Free*, examining the issue of equality for women in the church from a biblical perspective.

Because of that book, I have been exposed to the pain and joy of many women who, like me, were searching for answers about their place in this world and in God's family. I was asked to speak to organizations and at colleges and seminaries. And women wrote me letters. Everywhere I go they tell me how it is with them.

Because of my exposure to people on the front lines of change, I know some things. I know how it feels to hurt and be angry but have no one to talk to who understands. I know the self-doubts women harbor concerning their longing to use gifts and pursue dreams that have been forbidden to them. I know their sense of isolation. I know their feelings of desperation as they sit in situations that are tearing them apart inside.

And because I have been here and there talking to women in the pews, I have also been asked questions by those in positions of power and authority in the church. They want to know, some of them at least, what is going on. Some are genuinely puzzled by the intensity of the feelings that surface in some women when they are turned away from service or voice in the Church. Others, trying to be conciliatory but not wanting any kind of change, are genteel gentlemen, playing courteously dismissing games with me as they do with the women in their organizations and churches.

WHERE WE FIND OURSELVES JUST NOW

Nobody seems to put signs up on their church marquees denouncing feminism now, secular or otherwise. The issue has been successfully introduced as a valid subject for discussion in many churches. Not everywhere, it is true, but the general willingness to talk about the issue is a first step on the way to making change happen.

Talking about it does not mean, however, that something will actually *be done* about the issue. In most churches a holding action is taking place on the issue of woman's equal participation. Some denominations are using holding pattern tactics that are almost embarrassingly obvious. They set up study groups and committees to "look into the matter" and report in a year or two; then another committee is set up to "further look into the matter." This has gone on for several years and become obvious to large numbers of women within these denominations, who have subsequently and sorrowfully left for other churches and other denominations.

But even though this sad state of affairs forces painful choices on women who love their churches and want to stay but can no longer bear to, it is, in itself, a good sign. It says that (1) the issue is alive, (2) resistance is skimpy and unreliable (otherwise a holding pattern would not be necessary), and (3) eventually most people in the denomination will become embarrassed or disgusted by the transparent nature of the tactic and insist on change.

HISTORY PROGRESSES IN STAGES

I really love history. That wasn't always so. I remember being unimpressed with history classes in school because I am not number oriented, and it didn't really matter what year something happened in, at least not to me. If I had the century right, that was close enough. History seemed to be a dry recounting of what was done and when. It didn't have any real people in it.

But after I stopped going to school I rediscovered history on my own. I found that history is not about numbers at all, it's about people. I discovered how what people did interacted with factors such as weather and famine and fire, causing all sorts of startling results. I became fascinated by seventeenth-century England, and the effects of the Great Fire of London, and the Plague. And then I found that history has patterns. You can reach beneath the stories of people and their joys and tragedies and see *process*.

When I researched my first book, I discovered process at work in the movement of democracy toward equalizing opportunity for all people in this country. And I noticed the confluence of that democratic progress with other forces to produce issues that would come alive and stay alive until changes were made. One such issue is the contemporary issue of equality for women. It is especially interesting to see the confluence of influences at work in the case of equality for women in the Church.

The present rise of the prominence of hermeneutics (the art and science of Bible interpretation) in the Church coincides with a resurgence of the issue of equality for women in the secular world. Biblical evidences for women's place and participation have long been clouded by medievalist interpretations of Bible passages concerning women. But hermeneutics, making possible more accurate interpretations, has come to the forefront at just the time Christian women need good tools to find out what the Bible really says about them.

This process of history, observable in any time and on any subject, is at work in the changes in progress right now concerning women in the Church. It helps tremendously to know that. Something *is* happening. And it is happening in a predictable way. We can look at what has happened before and determine where we are at this time in the changemaking process. Knowing where we are will help us understand what we need to do to help ourselves as individuals caught up in the progress of events. It will also help us see how we might more smoothly make the changes we are seeking.

Where I see us now is just past the first stage of introducing the subject. People are taking us seriously now, some of them. Magazines and organizations who would never have asked me for my opinion on anything five years ago, except perhaps my roses or cookie recipes, now ask me for information and contributions.

This is wonderful progress—not necessarily for me, sometimes I might rather write about roses or cookies than equality for women. But it shows the progress of the issue through the changemaking process. Every change has to go through certain stages. We have passed the first one.

I suppose I should not say "passed" because change progresses unevenly. Some groups and some people move slowly. So while one group is now allowing women into the ordained ministry, another might still be trying to decide if they should allow discussion of the issue. But we are well enough into this stage to be ready in many places to go on to the next one. Even in the slow groups we can now look forward to a time when the next stage will be possible. (Though I should point out that there may be some who will hold out for a generation or more. One Protestant group was still denouncing the Copernican theory of the universe well into the latter half of the nineteenth century.)[1]

SUCCESSES

We are now at a leveling-off place. It is a good place to stop for a moment and recognize our successes.

We are talking about it. When I first began to write about equality for women in the church, people would call me on the phone and ask if they could come over and talk about the subject. They did so almost surreptitiously, fearful that what I might say would be outrageous or foolish. They wanted to believe there was something to what they had heard I believed and was writing, but they did not dare think it could actually be reasonable and true. So they didn't really want anyone else to know they were asking, not just yet, until they found out more.

And though college students are always hungry to hear about some subject just a little forbidden and seemingly iconoclastic, professors who dared have me, and others like me, speak to their classes or who sponsored seminars were in real danger of losing their jobs, or at least of coming up for criticism and warning. Now, however, it is a mark of reasonableness and fairmindedness in many schools to have "the Christian feminist" come on campus and speak. Since there aren't too many of us who can or will go about speaking, the variety to choose from is sort of small, and all who do speak receive many invitations. Because now it is the thing to do. And that's progress, one step in the changemaking process for those institutions and the people within them.

We are beginning to take ourselves seriously. Women always tend to suspect they are wrong when they get a new idea, or allow one they have been afraid of listening to to surface, and then do something about it. That is, of course, how we have been trained to be.

It takes time and thought and some tentative toe dampening in the waters of independence for women to take their own needs seriously. Then we aren't sure what to do about it. We are also afraid. And we are right to be afraid. Society in general, and certain individuals in particular, don't take kindly to uppity women who dare to be different and/or independent.

But, increasingly, more and more of us are coming to take ourselves seriously. We are beginning to believe we are real people with real needs, needs that do not automatically get met just because we are good girls. And that is *great* progress because change can only happen if we make it happen for us as individuals and then work together for collective change. But before we can make anything happen we have to take our needs seriously, and then take our power and strength and self-determination seriously too.

We are beginning to share and work together for what we want. Women are isolated from each other in today's world. Long ago women worked together on farms and in towns to bring babies into the world, nurse the sick, care for the old and the young, and share work. But the Industrial Revolution isolated us from one another just as it has isolated the generations from one another. As a result, we came, over time, to view other women as competition or as friends-at-a-distance, but not as co-workers.

That is changing as women realize they share so much in experience, feeling, and circumstance. Sometimes books are catalysts for bringing women back together. Women have told me they identify with me from reading my books. One told me she cried when she read about my experience weaning my child when I did not want to, she had been there too. Others have said, "I feel I know you." We are banding together and bonding together as women again, sharing our experiences and beginning to share the work again. And it feels very good.

WHAT THE PROBLEMS ARE

I am not going to balance the successes I have just mentioned with a section on failures, because I don't see it that way. We haven't failed because some things don't work as well as we would like. And we haven't failed because it is taking longer to get what we want than we thought it would. We are just experiencing problems that are natural to this changemaking process.

The major problem I see is that individual women are hurting badly.

They write to me, and they seek me out when I speak. And I, too, have been hurt.

In a changing social structure, fault lines develop between the opposing forces of the old and the new. Unfortunately, people get caught in those fault lines and become pressured, squeezed, and crushed. The cutting edge of social change has sharp teeth.

Women caught in pressure situations need to know that it is normal for this to happen. They probably didn't *do* anything to cause it, they were just at the right (or wrong) place at the right time. Believe it or not, knowing that *does* help some. We need to provide support and information for people so caught, and also help them recover from the damage when their ordeal is over.

Even though women are learning to work together as we have not done for a long time, we are unaccustomed to it and sometimes a bit clumsy. We need to learn how to cooperate and work together even better, and to use our resources for each other without the personal impoverishment of some balancing apathy in others.

Women experience a great deal of anger when they first become aware of the actual dimensions of their situation in the Church. We need to use that anger for good purposes, to allow it to burn itself out on worthwhile projects rather than turn it inward and let it burn us out inside, or turn it outward and hurt someone else.

Relationships with people, both men and women, who oppose equality for women are problems for many women. We need to know how to work through this conflict with people we care about but whose ideas and belief systems stifle and/or offend us.

One of the biggest problems women are experiencing is the pressure and pain they feel in their churches. They think they *must* go to church services. But increasingly, some of them find it almost impossible to do so. They really do not know what to do about this. And what they actually do is often self-destructive.

Another problem women face is that they do not know *how* to make changes. We are not routinely taught changemaking techniques as part of our growing up. We are taught, instead, to not make waves, to be peaceable, conciliatory, pliable, and cooperative with those who control our lives.

Women who want to make changes in their own lives, their churches, or the wider society usually have no idea how or where to begin. Unfortunately, they often imitate the changemaking strategies used on them by men or others who have power over them. These methods tend to be oppressive and confrontationist. And as such, they are severely limited in their scope of effectiveness. They also carry heavy personal and interpersonal disadvantages as well.

SEARCHING FOR SOLUTIONS

The first step in problem solving is always to determine what the problem is and who the problem actually belongs to. The next step is to search for all possible solutions. Wonderfully, the world is full of all sorts of people doing and trying new things, discovering how old things were actually done, and developing ways to do old things better.

Searching for solutions can be an exciting and pleasing activity. I hope to be able to put you in touch with ways to solve problems I mentioned. Some of these techniques adapt and apply themselves to such a wide range of problem solving and changemaking that you may find them changing your life in other areas as well.

Since people generate solutions in many different ways, the more people you can draw from the better your chances of finding useful techniques. I will share with you what I have found out from my own searching, from my contacts with others, and from observation.

THE CHURCH AS BODY

I am a Baptist by background and by persuasion. That is neither here nor there for many things (I am a Christian first). But one thing it does for me is it makes me unenamored with authoritarianism. I see the Church as a body of equal members. Rulers and officers only mean service and servants to me. I see the body of Christ on earth as a living organism with all its parts needing to work together as equals for that body to remain healthy.

Because of this, I know in my heart that the Church needs women, all of us, doing what God has given us as individuals. Not all jobs in the body are equally pleasant at the moment, but without them the whole thing would quickly become much more unpleasant. For example, coughing is important. So is vomiting, if something dangerous is down there and needs to come up. Right now the Church needs us to tell it where it needs to change. And maybe it isn't comfortable for us to tell, or for the Church to hear it. But to be healthy and whole, we need to tell, and the Church needs to listen. Then we need to take our rightful places ministering to each other from what God gives us to share.

What we are trying to do is keep the body that is the Church healthy and whole—to make it more whole than it has been since the first century. We want to restore its female components, not because they are female, but because they are people. Christ's body needs all his people.

THE AIM OF THIS BOOK

What I want to do in this book is share resources. Many people have written and talked to me. I will be quoting from some of their letters, while protecting their privacy. Resources also come from what I have learned through my own experiences as a Christian feminist. I learned some things the hard way—as you may not have to if I can share with you first. I've also learned by observing other people, both those working for equality and those opposing it.

Some of the things I want to share are specific changemaking techniques I have paid to learn from experts. You can use them to help you make personal changes in your own life. Some can also be used by groups to make changes in larger arenas.

WHO I HOPE WILL READ THIS BOOK

This is an insider's book. But it's an outsider's book too. I am not writing it just for women who want equality for women in the church. I am writing it for them, true, but not only for them.

There are many people who really don't understand what is happening to the women in their lives or in their churches, but they care, and they want to know. Who will tell them? Can they call up a feminist and say, "I am confused and puzzled. Why are these women acting this way? They never did before. And when I try to talk to them they get angry. Or they argue with me and try to convince me of something that seems all wrong to me." No, most of them can't do that. They do not know who to talk to. And even if they did, they would be in jeopardy of being insulted and lectured to.

I hope those people who want to know what is happening with women will read this book too. I will include material specifically for them in the hope that they will.

I also welcome to these pages pastors and men who have relationships with women caught up in wanting equality. I have specific information for you. I am going to assume you are people who care and who want to understand. I am also going to assume you have been victimized by some misplaced feminist anger too, because it is extremely likely that it has happened. I hope what I can share with you will make it easier for you to understand these women and to work with them to get what you both want.

Members of classes studying contemporary issues either in schools or in churches are welcomed readers. It is not enough to study only the Bible passages at issue. You cannot deal adequately with the subject until you look within the lives of women and see their searching, loss, and longing. You will also want to know *what* they intend doing about it and *how* they will go about it.

And, of course, I hope women who want to make changes toward full participation of women will read it. Women who want to share the experiences of others like them will also find what they are looking for here.

2. Meeting Your Own Needs

Years ago, as a very young teenager, I believed that women were created equal with men. There didn't seem to be anything I couldn't do if I really wanted to do it and if I felt that it would be pleasing to the Lord. I truly felt that life would be full of exciting, wonderful things for me. Still, in the back of my mind, I thought this wonderful life would come through some man.

I married, hoping to share someone's wonderful future. I thought I could just sit back and wait for this wonderful life to come to me. Needless to say, it never arrived. After ten years of waiting, frustration, and depression, I was ready to give up. I actually asked the Lord to give me this wonderful life I had waited for or else to take my life away . . .

Finally, after all those years, I realized that if I sat around waiting for life to come to me, I'd be waiting forever. . . . I'm beginning to see that not only must I make my own life, but I can make it what I really want it to be.

A strange thing about women and their efforts for change is that they tend to forget the most important people in the whole scheme— themselves. A woman in a difficult relationship tends to focus on her partner. In a family, she focuses on the other members, or on the most needy member. In a society, women focus on other groups, almost never on themselves. We, who want change, whose lives are so immediately and constantly affected by the present situations we want changed, leave ourselves out of the reality/change picture.

However, confronting reality and effecting change require taking ourselves into account. So I am beginning this book with the chief item of business all women must take up to make change happen and to successfully deal with our realities—ourselves. Not ourselves *en masse,* but ourselves one by one, our *own* selves as individuals. You and me.

A few years ago I sat in the office of the president of Moody Bible Institute, a meeting arranged at my request, but for his benefit. In those days I was doing everything within my strength, and sometimes considerably beyond it, to meet the needs of and to be helpful to everyone who asked me or who appeared to need me.

I had been working at my jobs of writing, homemaking, and mothering three teenagers and one preteen, a sometimes stressful combination of activities. In addition I was taking speaking engagements that depleted my reserves and stressed me further. Because of one of those speaking engagements, I was here in this man's office trying to be helpful again.

The controversy about the Equal Rights Amendment was heating up locally, with "Stop ERA" activists hard at work in churches throughout the Chicago area. In my city—Wheaton, Illinois—some of them noticed a newspaper item announcing that I would be speaking to a local group called Housewives for ERA. The notice mentioned some places I had previously spoken, Moody Bible Institute among them. It also mentioned where my husband was employed, again, Moody Bible Institute. The "Stop ERA" women, about six of them, attended the meeting.

I did not talk about ERA during the course of my speech. My subject was that of my book *Woman Be Free*, biblical equality for women in the Church. The "Stop ERA" women dominated the whole of the question-and-answer period afterward with questions about my own views on the Equal Rights Amendment and other subjects they considered relevant.

My candid and honest answers, distorted into other forms and meanings, appeared a few days later in letters to Moody Bible Institute executives. The letters denounced me and my husband (for his association with me) as being pro-homosexuality, eager to send our daughter to battle, and doubting the truth of the Bible.

Since I had no idea what was going on, I began trying to track down the letter writers to find out. From a guest book signed at the meeting, I got a list of new names, then made phone calls to ask if any of them had written the letters.

Some of the women admitted what they had done. When I pointed out the defamatory and unfair nature of the letters, one said anything they did to me was justified because ERA would destroy our society. Their intent with the letters, they said, was not to hurt me but to force Moody to make a policy statement against ERA (something Moody did not, and could not reasonably do, since it is an institution with radio stations, a magazine, etc.). One of the women gave a copy of her letter to a local minister, who photocopied, distributed it at his church and elsewhere, and broadcast parts of it on his radio program. He asked listeners to write to Moody and complain and threaten to withhold financial support.

So I asked for a meeting with Moody's president. I wanted to share my information about the source of the letters with him because I was sure he was as puzzled by them as I had been. I knew that he would undoubtedly be asked questions about the supposed situation (errant professor and wife) on his travels for the school. I wanted to provide him with accurate answers and save him from embarrassment.

I didn't think he or anyone at Moody would take the letters seriously. The writers did not even agree among themselves about what I had said and done. And I was sure those at the Institute knew my husband and my writing well enough to know the outrageous claims were false.

After I told the president my findings, he and the dean of education, who had also received letters and asked to be a part of the meeting, said they understood the situation and indicated they did not take the letters seriously. But, they said, they did want to discuss some things with me. What they *were* concerned about was my beliefs about equality for women in the Church.

After explaining what I did believe and the biblical evidence I based it on, I said to the president, "Is it what I believe about women and the Bible that you are concerned about, or where it might lead?" The president said, "It's about where it might lead." I said, "Where are you afraid it might lead?" He said, "I don't know."

They then said they were concerned that someone might associate my work with their institution. I said, no, I never allowed such association to be made. Most people I spoke to and wrote for did not even know my husband taught there. (I realized only later that these men seemed totally unable to see me as a writer, but only as the wife of one of their professors.) And when I was asked about Moody's policy on the issue, I always praised Moody, said I had no connection there, and that it was a place I respected.

They still were not comfortable with my work in this area. The president said, "You are talented, why don't you do something else?" I, shamefully courteous, even in the face of such outrageous condescension (they did not even realize it was such, giving every appearance of advising an innocent who had stepped out of the bounds of propriety), said that writing was what I wanted to do, that they had nothing to fear from my work, it did not involve the school.

I remembered that I had a newspaper interview coming up in a few days. So I thought I could reassure them by explaining how I would answer if questions were asked about Moody in the interview. (There was no reason to expect that any would be because it was to be a simple "local author, human interest" piece.) I told them that if any were asked I would speak well of the Institute and disassociate myself from it. Their response was "Maybe you should not go through with the interview."

I naively thought this was just a case of institutional caution and lack of knowledge on their part about author interviews. But it wasn't a suggestion to a writer. It was, as I realized later, a command to someone they assumed was under the command of someone under their command. Shortly after the interview appeared, I was officially banned from all radio, publications, and speaking on campus at the Institute. The vice-president issuing the memo admitted to my husband that they did not even read the interview. My allowing it was enough.

The letters kept coming in, denouncing people the writers did not know for things that had not happened and words that had not been said. Moody fired my husband—to maintain face, I suppose, though actually it lost face through it's shameful treatment of the man. I was not present at the meeting in which this deed was accomplished, even though I asked to be. It was all really about me, but I was invisible through the whole sequence of events, merely a vehicle for the playing out of a scenario of slander and libel, power and money—and expendability. And I, doing what women have done down through history, was there through it all, expending myself being helpful.

And that's the way it is with all of us. We are weighted under the load of oppression, and even as we struggle and work to heave it off our collective backs we forget about our own individual back. It can break under the load, and we won't even think to prevent it or minimize the damage, or even take adequate steps for recovery. We are invisible in our perception of reality and change.

But in order to change the things we want changed and to deal with reality realistically, we have to become visible to ourselves. We have to learn to provide for ourselves. Contrary to all our training, we must learn to meet our own needs.

WOMEN ARE UNSUITED BY LIFE EXPERIENCE FOR MEETING THEIR OWN NEEDS

In a war-oriented society, which ours is, one needs men always available who will do as they are told, suffer injury and death for some vague cause or at some leader's command, and detach themselves from feeling and kin to do so. From the beginning, little boys are trained to be good soldiers. Their games and socialization follow in line with that objective.

Little girls are trained, from the beginning, to be good mothers— also quite important in a war-oriented society. Whatever else we do with our lives, that early training is present. And we as women have the behaviors and skills that result from such training.

A good mother provides for her child first and for herself second. She cares about other people's needs. She empathizes and discerns needs without being told. She will wait, putting aside her own wants, longings, and needs for even elemental requirements such as sleep and food and clothing until the child is safe, well, and fed. Mothers *then* try to catch up on their own needs if and when the opportunity comes.

Women, as a part of this socialization, also believe that if they behave as they are taught to, if they are *good,* everything will work out well in the end. The right man will come along, the man will protect them, the war will be over, the crop will be harvested, the child will recover. Women are taught that if they behave as good mothers they will be taken care of *by someone who has more power than they do.*

We all believe this. We may not know we believe it, but look at our actions and you can see that we do. When I, being helpful, tried to meet everyone else's needs except my own I risked myself, squandered myself for people who did not have my best interests at heart. But I, intent on being good and helpful, did not allow myself to suspect that. I believed that if I was a good girl good men would treat me right. Even as a logical, practical feminist I believed that somewhere down inside. I did not have within my behavioral repertoire choices I needed to provide adequately for myself.

In order for us to go about making the changes we want in our society and church and individual lives, we will have to learn new behaviors. Many of those behaviors have to do with meeting our own needs.

CHANGING OUR FOCUS

Women in disadvantageous marriage relationships, in bad work situations, in uncomfortable relationships of all kinds typically think in terms of changing the oppressor. The reason many battered wives stay with their batterers is that they keep thinking, "If only he would change." Women whose children treat them with disrespect and disdain think, "If only I can teach them to treat me better—oh, if only they would." Wives of alcoholics focus on the man and his drinking, allowing the whole family to rotate around an axis of alcohol.

Since I first became aware of this phenomenon, I began telling women who asked my advice to stop focusing on the other side, and to focus instead on their own lives and needs and wants. I have noticed a recurrent response; they seem to awaken from a dream. They say, "But can I really do that? Is it OK?" And then they realize that, of course, it is OK—they are *people,* adults. They have a right to a life, a life that is theirs alone. Then changes begin to happen, and it is the women who make them happen. They are no longer waiting for someone else to change, in order to change their own lives.

In this chapter, I want to do two things. I want to impress upon you as well as I know how the necessity for us to learn to meet our own needs. Then I want to share some specific techniques and suggestions about how to do that. As we move on to fullness of opportunity, we need to move on as whole persons.

DETERMINE WHAT YOUR NEEDS ARE

Women have a hard time knowing what their real needs are. We tend to think so much in terms of self-sacrifice that many, if not most, of us think that wanting something for ourselves is automatically suspect. Several women have asked me about writing. They would love to write. How does one go about it? Are they being silly to think they can? And at least two very capable women have insisted (and I believe them) that they are afraid to write *because* they want to. They say they don't know if they are *supposed to* write. They believe that God must give them some sign or calling and they must have a specific subject they feel called to write about in order to justify doing it. These women would not say that about other activities they choose every day. But those choices can be justified as necessary or helping other people. Writing is something they want so very much to do that they are suspicious about it. Only a strong indication that *God* wants them to do it would override that suspicious hesitation. I seriously doubt that men are as oppressed with this kind of self-denying overscrupulousness as women are.

Women link the self-searching question "Can you justify this expenditure?" to all manner of personal choices. It's the mother training again. So you may have to work at digging out your needs and convincing yourself that it is OK to meet them. Let me remind you that you really *are* a fully human being. The world may deny that with its restrictions and training, but it *is* true. You must reeducate yourself to act on that truth.

Get a notebook. I'm a believer in writing it down because that works for me. If I try to carry all I want to do, all I have discovered, and all I want to be sure and remember in my head at the same time all the time, I drop things out of my mental basket. So I write them down. And I recommend it to you as a way to help you learn to meet your own needs.

Make this notebook your self-discovery notebook, your self-education, self-recovery, self-enhancement, self-nourishing book. Write your discoveries, wonderings, enlightenments—whatever seems to want to be there in it. Begin by listing your needs. Leave plenty of room to add entries as you discover more or discover refinements and insight on what is already there.

You need what you feel you need. You don't need what you are supposed to need, or what someone else thinks or feels you need, or what your friends or relatives need. You don't need what seems logical that you should need, or any other discounting, distorting assessment. You need what *you* *think* and/or *feel* you need. If you feel it, write it down. Figure it out later.

You may surprise yourself here. I've been keeping a notebook for some time. At first I wrote down such items as more time for myself, clothing I would really like rather than what I was actually buying (strange practice, dressing differently from the way we want to), someone to talk to who would really listen. Then I began writing down things I wanted for myself that I intended to get from other people, things I was going to insist on. But now I find I am reaching beneath the specifics and realizing that I have some large, and encompassing needs, basic needs that involve both people and specifics.

One of those needs is for security. I have had a keen sense of recognition that I need to *feel* secure. I realized that I had always counted on other people to give me that security, but that often they hadn't done it or been able to do it. So I determined to discover how to provide, as much as is possible, my own security. And my first step, interestingly enough, was to refer myself back to meeting my own needs. Making sure you have the things you need provides security.

After you have written down what you need, *think about what it means.* I like to think of this part of the need-meeting process as "simmering." Are there implications, areas to explore here? Explore them. Insights resulting? Maybe you will want to write them down. This kind of thinking can lead you into areas you need to go, producing insightful and enlightening discoveries about yourself and how you relate to work, play, about other people, etc.

Set in motion the obvious. Find someone who *will* listen when you talk. Go alone, or with a friend. Enjoy your children separately, in your own way, if it's not like your husband's way. Begin studying what you have wanted to learn. Make plans for new directions. Choose the first step forward and do it.

Continue the process. Ask yourself as you go to sleep at night and as

you wake up in the morning, *"How can I meet my own needs?"* Listen
to what your own inner voice tells you. Then act in your own behalf.

DISCOVER YOUR PARTS

One of the problems with being female is that we "aren't all here."
We've been told that we aren't all here for so long that we believe it
unconsciously even if we don't believe it consciously. We have not been
allowed to be all here for so long that we don't know what's missing.
I have a technique to remedy that. It works very well. I call it discovering your parts.

When I say "parts," realize that this is only a way of talking about
who we are in all our inner diversity. In some ways, each one of us
is more like a committee than a single person. At least it helps to think
of it that way. One part may want to go out and change the world,
while another part would rather take a good book out behind the house
and eat chocolates and let the world change itself, thank you. We can
genuinely want both those things at the same time. That's what's called
Inner Conflict. Discovering your parts helps cut down considerably on
conflicts between differing desires and wants. It also is wonderful for
discovering who we are in all our richness. It helps satisfy those
longings that we can't quite put a name to, answering the lost voices
that call to us to do *something*, we don't quite know what.

Make a parts list. Take out your notebook and begin a new page or
section with a heading: PARTS LIST, or whatever you want to call
it. Then begin listing all the parts you recognize as who you are. Name
and describe each one briefly, or more lengthily, as you wish, noting
what they do for you and what they want.

Make sure you list your parts in positive terms. You may be inclined
to give some of them negative names and descriptions or decide you
don't like them very much. But you will almost certainly find, when
you become better acquainted with those parts, that they are doing their
best to do something good for you. They may not be doing it the way
you would like, or as well as you can train them to, but they're trying.

It's a good idea to select a time and place for parts listing when and
where you can be alone without interruption for a half hour or more.

You need a certain amount of peace and quiet to do an inner search like this.

As an example, a parts list might contain:

Holly Homemaker——loves to clean, enjoys the look, feel, and smell of a clean bathroom, freshly washed windows, coordinates wallpaper and curtains, makes beds smoothly, loves coziness and order. Wants results she can see, smell, and touch.

Laid Backer——drops clothing on chairs, eats cereal out of the box with her hands, watches TV, goes barefoot, admires cats. Wants to feel good, be lazy.

Spiritual Quester——loves to sit and think, look for deep meaning in experiences and understand life. Wants to do something meaningful and lasting, reach out to others and touch souls.

All Business Annie——no nonsense, she gets the job done. "Don't bother me with useless details!" She's on time, direct. Wants to cut out unnecessary red tape and eliminate waste. Would like to own her own business, make a lot of good clean money.

Keep on listing parts as you discover them, noticing how each one feels, what she wants, longs for, would like to have. Leave space to add to your list in future sessions as you discover more parts or that some parts actually are more than one part combined, that you can separate for better satisfaction.

Satisfy all your parts. You will probably recognize immediately that some of your parts have been short-changed. Other parts are getting more than their share of your resources and attention.

I found recently that my Servant part which does the things that have to get done, that no one (including me) particularly wants to do, had taken over many jobs that other parts could enjoy if allowed to do the work in their own way. So I am in the process of redistribution and rediscovery of how I can enjoy more of the things I do. My part that I call The Cozy Cottager actually can enjoy cleaning the bathroom if she doesn't have to do it too often and can do it her own way, making it look nice and pretty, taking her time, and stopping to enjoy how it all looks when she is done.

Redistribute your time and efforts to satisfy the parts that are being left out or left with too little. Allow yourself the joy and satisfaction of being wholly satisfied. You will find that if you check your parts list often, even daily for a while, and make sure all parts have a way to be satisfied, that you will have a feeling of completeness and peaceful vitality you may not have experienced since the freedoms of childhood. People I have recommended parts listing and satisfying to have commented on this good feeling.

Now for the seemingly negative parts. Ask inwardly what they are trying to do for you. A critical part that is always telling you what is wrong may be trying to protect you from the criticisms of others, maybe from criticisms provided by someone in your past. If you recognize that is the case, give the part something worthwhile to do for you *now* instead. You might tell yourself, and that part, that it no longer needs to say those words to you, but it can watch for times when you need to stop and think about what you are doing, saying, or feeling to determine if you need to do something different. Such a part may even be trying to protect you from overwork or over vulnerability in situations and with people who are not safe for you.

To resolve day-to-day inner conflicts, take out your parts list and ask if two or more parts are in conflict about something. For example, one part wants to protect you from overwork and another part wants to go out and work for the cause. Negotiate with the parts until you can find a way to satisfy all that are involved. Some may be willing to wait if they know their interests are being well served and not disregarded.

You might think of your different parts as checks and balances within to make sure you do what is best for you. Whenever you cooperate with your inner diversity and help work out a division of labor and privilege that satisfies all parts you will find that you operate much more smoothly and get more done that pleases you, in every area.

Not every part will want something every day. So only do what wants doing. Ask what is wanted and needed, and provide.

I know parts listing and negotiation may sound unusual at first. But if you think about it, it makes sense. By holding much of what we know and care about outside of conscious awareness but retrievable, we are able to operate more efficiently and comfortably. And if you need proof that unconscious parts exist, think about this: you have a part that knows how to keep you from falling off the bed while you are asleep. It has been there since early childhood. It does its job well. The rest of you can sleep, but it, in a sense, stays awake quietly protecting you.

GIVE YOURSELF A FUTURE

Women think their futures will be taken care of by other people. As girls we, for a time, believe that we have futures that we can determine. But most of us come to understand sometime around or just after adolescence that we are the only ones who have taken our own determination of our futures seriously. It is assumed that a husband will determine a woman's future. Oh, she will *help* in decision making, but she will live where his work takes him, even if she has work of her own. And her children will determine her future; then possibly her, or her husband's parents, who may need care someday.

Even women who believe they are independent and self-determining people often have a poor sense of their own future. They do not have a future that is *real* to them, only a *hoped for* future, one with vague outlines in their minds, longed for but fuzzy and ill defined.

This lack of a future that is real to us makes it extremely hard for us to bring about the changes we want. In order to gain something, you need to be able to have a full representation of it in your mind. Otherwise, you will not have a way to determine the steps toward it because you will not know *in sensory detail* exactly where you are going. That is not to say that one must have a complete *list* of what one wants. It is to say that if you do not have a *real sense* of your future and what it can hold for you, you can't get it.

How can you make your future real to you?

You must be able to see it. Visualize what you long for as if it were already an accomplished fact. How will you *look* in that future? What kind of clothing will you wear? How will you stand, sit? What will you surround yourself with that looks different from now? Make a picture of your future, the one you want for yourself, whenever you are working on meeting your needs.

You must know how it will sound. What will your voice be like saying the things you will say, need to say, want to say in the future that you want for yourself? How will other people speak to you? How will you respond? What speech will you react to differently then from the way you do now? How will you react then?

You must know how it will feel. If you have made a visual image of your desired future and added sound, add feeling. How will you feel in these situations in the future you want for yourself? How will you feel as you move through the actions you have visualized? Feel that feeling now.

Practicing a future desired state will make it possible for you to automatically make fine distinctions between where you are now and where you want to go, making many small choices at the appropriate moments to create the future you want.

Tie your real future image to a phrase, an object, or a visual cue. I borrowed a cue phrase from a videotaped changemaking therapy session. The young woman on the tape wants to give herself a new set of behaviors that will make possible her goal. At one point she says, "I deserve better," realizing that it is not only OK for her to achieve her goal but that she deserves what she wants rather than what she has. She later uses the phrase to remind herself of this knowledge. It represents her whole new orientation, and as such it calls into view a full representation of the future she wants. It also gives her a standard by which to judge her treatment of herself.

I have found her phrase, "I deserve better," a helpful cue for me in my own personal changemaking. When I am confronted with a situation I do not want, but that I have tolerated, I now remind myself, *I deserve better.* I then adjust my actions to reflect my commitment to a now much more real future that I do deserve.

The cue could be a visual image you have to remind you of how you will look in your desired future. It could be an object you carry in your purse, that sits on your desk, or hangs on the wall. It can be something you already have and attach new meaning to, something you make or clip from a newspaper or magazine, or buy purposefully as a talisman or token representing what you want for your future.

Practice making your future real, and it will be.

TAKE CARE OF YOUR PAST IN THE PRESENT

We all have traumas. You really can't grow up without any. When you venture into the arena of changemaking, you may activate old trauma feelings and wounds by the stresses you encounter in your new activities. Many women who are trying to be change agents in the church repeatedly overstress themselves. Daring to do things new and frightening to them, they take on responsibilities and tasks that are heavily loaded with emotional freight and enter situations ripe with potential for abuse and discouragement.

These new stresses can reactivate and intensify stress reactions from the past. We can call it burnout or overwork, or just stress. But whatever we call it, many of us need help with it.

I've had my share of this stress–distress. My eventual response (I had to do something, I felt I was becoming immobilized by it) was to read voraciously about the subject. I then experimented with different stress reduction methods and ways to defuse the past to find out what would work for me.

In the Resources section of this book, I have included a list of books on the subject that I found most helpful. But here and now I want to give you some techniques that will work for you now to reduce the stresses that result from your work for equality for women. They will also work on old, long-submerged hurts as well.

Humans process information in discernible patterns. Understanding those patterns makes it possible to change the effects of our experiences and memories. Several effective techniques for such change have been developed in the last few years. I'll be sharing the techniques that I know work from my own experience with them. I've gathered them from many sources, from books, personal consultation with change-making experts, and some are innovations of my own.

CHANGE YOUR INNER MESSAGES

One thing that causes inner pain is the replaying of inner destructive messages. Some of these messages we are aware of, some we are not. You can short-circuit them and empty them of their power by *changing the message.* If you remember over and over again words or conversations from your past (whether it was long ago or last night) that cause you pain, say to yourself whenever the memory comes again, "That was then and there, this is here and now." Or, if it was something someone else said or is from someone else's influence, say, "Those are not my words, those are his (or her) words."

Whenever the memory intrudes again, repeat the phrase immediately. You will thus link them together in your mind and the uncomfortable message will first fade and eventually stop entirely.

Another way to remove unpleasant feelings from a remembered message is to mentally replay it in several distorted forms, in succession. Replay it in each of the following ways: speed it up, then make it very slow. Use a high pitched voice, then a low pitched voice. Imagine listening to it spoken by a Donald Duck voice, and any other inappropriate sounding voice.

CHANGE THE PICTURE

If the uncomfortable memory takes a visual form, you can also alter the picture itself to change its effect.

1. If you see the experience from your own vantage point *within* the action (as a performer in a play), change it by stepping outside the picture. Take the position of a bystander from a distance observing the action (as someone watching a play or movie), observing yourself when you were a part of it. In other words, you are watching a younger you in the experience rather than watching the experience from within the action.

2. Dull any colors, dim the lighting, and blur outlines. Make it a fainter image.

3. See it as happening further away. Make it a smaller picture. Send it further and further away into the distance until it is only a small dot. You might even make the dot so small that it disappears.

Experiment with this technique to see what works best for you. Some people find that adding happy background music or circus music to the mental picture changes the whole thing for them. Try changing the picture in different ways and notice how it affects how you feel about it.[2]

CHANGE THE FEELING BY CHANGING BREATHING AND POSTURE

When you experience discouragement, anxiety, or depression, you can change that feeling by changing the breathing patterns and postures you tend to assume in such states. Adding the phrase, "I choose *this* feeling instead," at the moment you change breathing and posture, can make this method even more effective.

Feelings we commonly think of as negative—depression, anxiety, fear, discouragement, and remorse—pair with a curled-over, downward-looking posture, and with shallow breathing and momentarily holding one's breath. By changing your physiology, you can change your state.

Experiment to see where and how you breathe when you feel the way you want to feel, or in the state you want to exchange for negative ones. Determine the components of your optimal state of well-being, of calmness, and confidence. Notice how you hold your body, where your eyes look (higher or lower at objects in front of you). Use that posture and breathing as a reference point for a resource state to adopt whenever you want to change from an unwanted feeling state.

To do this, say to yourself, "I choose *this* feeling instead," and change to the preferred state's breathing pattern and posture. Usually an upright posture with chest, head, and chin held high and eyes looking higher than shoulder level will go with the middle and upper chest breathing of an optimal state.

BURN OFF ADRENALIN

A psychologist friend of mine prescribes whacking a bed with a tennis racquet and "vocalizing" while you do it to use up the extra adrenalin stress produces. The adrenalin is there to make fight or flight possible. But since neither reaction is appropriate for most of our stress-producing situations, we accumulate its troubling physiological effects. She also encourages kicking a pillow placed on the floor in the corner of a room, pounding a pillow with your fists, twisting a towel (wringing it violently with both hands), running, walking, punching a punching bag, and biting a wet washcloth (careful here if you have fragile dental work). These are good first-aid methods for relieving accumulated tension.

Another method, which sounds funny, but which does work, is moaning and groaning. For this, you will need enough privacy to avoid alarming your family and neighbors. Or perhaps you could get them to join you. Moaning and groaning is done lying on the floor—rolling about, if you like. Or it can be done in the shower, or while walking —wherever you have enough auditory privacy. Actually, moaning and groaning usually ends up being funny. Maybe the laughter is part of why it works.

GET REGULAR LARGE-MUSCLE EXERCISE

Although researchers don't know exactly why, depressed people recover as well or better with aerobic exercise therapy as they do with antidepressive drugs. Exercise may work so well at making people feel good because it produces endorphins in the brain. Endorphins are euphoria-producing substances we manufacture after about twenty minutes of aerobic exercise (such as brisk walking, running, bicycling, swimming). And—unlike drugs, endorphins have no disadvantageous side effects.

Besides making you feel good mentally, regular exercise using your large muscles keeps your whole body in tone. It promotes sound sleep and helps you withstand stress. So to do the *best* for yourself, you need to exercise regularly.

I prefer walking and using a minitrampoline for inventing my own dancing, jumping, armswinging free-form exercise to music. I also use a rowing machine sometimes when I watch TV. I figure that if I'm going to watch a tension-producing news program, I might as well do something to reduce the tension at the same time instead of sitting passively through it.

I also stop periodically during the day while I am writing or working at something else and do a few minutes of walking, rowing, or exercising on the minitrampoline.

Lest I falsely appear to be a paragon of fitness, I will reveal that I do not do all these activities all the time. And sometimes I don't do any of them for a while. But when I don't, I can tell the difference, not only in my body, but in my stress level. And I return to them eventually and resolve to keep doing them.

Begin at the easiest point for you. Do what you find most pleasurable. It will be worth your efforts.

NEUTRALIZE UNCOMFORTABLE ASSOCIATIONS

Memories and experiences are laid on neural pathways that are sensorily specific. So you remember not only in three dimensional color, but you also remember how things smelled, sounded, tasted, and felt. Whenever you remember a particularly good experience fully, you feel the same feelings in your body you felt when it first happened. That is partly how you remember—you re-experience it to some extent each time. You also remember unpleasant experiences the same way, re-experiencing the unpleasant feelings. And that, of course, is the problem.

Technique 1.

Because of *how* we remember, we can modify a bad memory by purposefully creating a specific good memory and tying it to the bad one by a simple linking technique. By linking them together, the good memory neutralizes the bad one.

First, purposefully construct a good memory. You can create one in your imagination to use at any time in your future. This created memory-experience can be used over and over again. You do not have to make a new one for each negative memory-feeling you want to neutralize. You will be creating an all-purpose neutralizer. So make it a really nice one.

For example, sit comfortably, and imagine being in a beautiful place. If you love the seashore, you could imagine a beach complete with sand, seagulls, water, sea air, and sun. Choose a place of your own preference. Be there in your imagination. Notice how the air there feels on your skin. Feel the breeze as it moves your hair gently. Notice the smell of the air, the sea, whatever is there. Look all around you. Be aware of the sounds that are natural to the surroundings, even if the sound is peaceful silence.

When you are fully aware of and enjoying your created place, clasp one wrist with the other hand and hold it firmly but gently for several seconds while you continue to enjoy your created experience.

Now, release the grip on your wrist and return to your immediate surroundings here and now. Look around the room to reorient yourself. Again clasp your wrist with your hand *just as you did while experiencing your imaginary surroundings*. (The same wrist as before, in exactly the same way.)

You will find that the physical clasping of your wrist brings back the beautiful place and a full enjoyment of the created experience again. Sit and hold your wrist for a few more seconds and enjoy the experience fully again.

To more firmly associate the experience with your hand-wrist touch, repeat the process of unclasping your wrist and noticing your present surroundings to re-orient yourself to here and now, and then clasping your wrist to recall the created experience. Do this two or three times to firmly establish the neurological connections.

You now have an all-purpose neutralizer to use to help you with feelings you do not want. You can also use it to help you relax, go to sleep, or just feel pleasant. Whenever a negative memory or feeling intrudes, simply grasp your wrist *in exactly the same way* as when establishing the neutralizing experience, and hold it for several seconds. You will find that the negative memory will lose some of its power to bring the negative feelings to you. You will still be able to remember it, but it will not have the same power anymore. By repeatedly using this neutralizer, the memory will eventually be *only* a memory, without the negative feelings.

What is actually happening is that two neurological pathways with opposite feelings have been blended together. The effect is to weaken the intensity of the one with negative feelings. Use your neutralizing created experience whenever and wherever you wish. You can establish others in the same way. Any touch can be used to activate it. A clasping of the wrist is easy and unobtrusive—no one but you will know what you are doing.

Technique 2.

Make a mental black-and-white movie of the experience that carries unpleasant feelings or memories for you. But watch this mental movie as though you were sitting in a movie theater. In other words, you are seeing the action from the bystander's vantage point.

Run the movie to the end, through the whole episode, and freeze the final frame as a slide.

Now imagine yourself leaving your seat in the theater, moving up to the screen, and entering that final frame. You now will be seeing things as they looked from inside, as a participant rather than as a bystander.

Turn the action back on and run the movie backward at high speed. Do it very quickly, taking only a few seconds. And this time make it in full color instead of black and white.[3]

These techniques change the mental associations we have with past experiences. Rather than up-close, as if we were re-experiencing them, they help us see them in perspective, as at a distance.

LEARN TO SAY YES TO YOURSELF AND NO TO OTHERS

In the stage play and movie *Oklahoma,* Ado Annie sang, "I'm jest a gal who cain't say no!" Most of the rest of us gals "jest cain't say no" either. Oh, we may be able to resist the advances of peddlers and cowboys for hugs, kisses, and further entanglements, unlike Annie. But for most things, we "cain't say no" to hardly anyone but ourselves.

I find that I can say no to myself when I want new clothes much easier than I can say no to my children when they want some new item to wear. I can stay up late to wash clothes they didn't mention until bedtime that they needed the next day. I can bake cookies when I need to do something else (or would just plain rather not), I can work on committees, talk on the phone with someone, go to the market, you name it. I have trouble saying no.

I don't think I'm the exception either. Let's face it, we were trained to be that way. Good girls don't stamp their little feet, put out their lower lip, and say, No! They smile, and like the Little Engine That

Could, say, "I think I can, I think I can, I hope!" Almost every one of us at least tried to be a good girl.

To make it worse, we learned to never say no to the people in authoritarian positions over us, particularly Daddy. When we grew up and went out in the world, we found that almost every person in any position superior to ours (and that's most of them) is a man acting like Daddy when he didn't want to have anyone tell him no. So we consistently try harder, do more, and get less for ourselves.

What we have to do is practice, practice, practice so we can say no to *anyone*. But that won't, in itself, solve the problem. We will also have to practice, practice, practice saying yes to ourselves until we can do that comfortably too. You can use the following technique to help you say no to others and yes to yourself.

Remember the last time you should have said no, but didn't. Go back in your imagination and look at that situation again. But this time make the changes in yourself that you would need to be able to say no. For example, if you needed courage, give your imaginary self that resource.

In your imaginary restructuring of the episode, notice the way you would sit, stand, move, speak, and look with the courage you needed. Make adjustments to the scene, adding any other needed resources in the same manner until you are satisfied and comfortable with it.

Now replay the whole experience the new way with added resources. See it in your mind's eye as it would have been if you had all you needed to be able to say no. Notice the way the courageous (or whatever resources you added) you feels in the new version. Feel that feeling now.

Next, select a future possible situation in which you will need this resource to be able to say no. Make a mental movie of that future experience with the added resources making it possible for you to say no.

Select one or two more future possible situations and do the same with them too.

Follow the same steps to mentally practice saying yes to yourself.

This has been a long chapter, full of all sorts of things. Some people reading this may wonder why some of it is here. Do we really need to know about exercise and neutralizing negative memories? Well, yes. If you don't need it now, then you probably haven't had any bad changemaking experiences yet. But if you have had such experiences, then you know why these items are here. And you are probably already using some of them, even before finishing the chapter. Changemaking is a big job, and a sometimes bloody one. You need all the help you can get. I know that because I've been there, and because I have seen the wounded.

Please give yourself the option of taking your own self and your own needs seriously. We can free our individual selves at the same time we work to free ourselves as a group. We will never be free as a group until we are free individually.

3. Meeting Needs Together

... I have said all that in order to say this: thank you. While reading your books I have felt that spark of recognition—that feeling of hope that comes when you realize that someone else has been there—that you are not all alone in the world after all.

Frankly, for most of my life I stifled my giftedness and I was so afraid of that side of myself that I hid it from everyone, even members of my own family. . . .

When I began, years ago, asking questions about women's unequal participation in the Church, I thought I was the only one who wanted to know, the only one who minded being a second-class citizen in the Church. Pastors I asked my innocent questions of dismissed them with an indulgent smile, gave quick, inadequate answers and changed the subject or escaped—or they rudely put me down and insulted me for asking. The implication was almost always that there must be something wrong with me for not being satisfied with the strange and puzzling unequal state of affairs—*other* women were content, why wasn't I? I thought I was all alone.

And I thought that until I began to understand the great silence behind which women hide their secret longings and fears. I began to suspect I was not alone. But I wasn't sure. Not until I began writing and then speaking on the subject of equality for women in the Church. Then I discovered we are everywhere. Scattered about, here one, there two or three, but scattered *everywhere.*

You are not alone. And though one can changemake quite well and effectively all by oneself, there are advantages to banding together both to changemake and to meet needs together.

We are isolated from each other by many barriers, separated by our allegiances, our lack of ways to communicate, lack of opportunity and knowhow, and by fear.

This was not always so. From beyond history women have worked together, supported each other in need, and been resources for each other, teaching, helping, and sharing. That is, up until the Industrial Revolution.

Before the Industrial Revolution, most work was family business and the work site was also the home site. Families were large and multigenerational. They might include serving maids, field hands, cousins, aunts, or others attached to the place of work/home. In such a setting, children were cared for by available adults. Children were in contact with a broad range of people, male and female, throughout the day. They also learned the family business. Women worked together and together with men in the family business and in the business of the family.

In such settings women shared much work. Large numbers of people in close working conditions, and the need to produce a wide range of goods and services, made it natural to do so. Growing up on a farm in Arkansas, I had a chance to take part in such a lifestyle even though the time was considerably after the Industrial Revolution. Women worked together to can fruits and vegetables, make quilts, assist at the birth of babies, and provide food after funerals and threshings. My mother was the sixth of seven daughters in a family of nine children. Her common maxims reflect her upbringing. She would sometimes say to my brother and me, "Many hands make light work," to encourage us to work. Of course, two pairs of hands are not "many." But she grew up listening to that saying, and it was demonstrably true then. That is the way women used to learn, work, and share.

They don't do it that way anymore. And because they don't we have forgotten how. We feel all alone. While they work together women talk about the things that are on their minds. When they are in a strictly social setting, they talk about a more stylized set of subjects; they are *nice* then, courteous, *careful,* closed. When we stopped working together, we lost a way of sharing our deepest concerns. We also lost a way of sharing our resources with each other.

We must learn how to do that again. We are learning. We are discovering how to meet needs together, our own and the needs in a wider circle that can take in the whole world.

FINDING EACH OTHER

We need ways to find each other, to touch and get together, if we want to. At the least we need a way to share information that is reliable and regular. I am hoping this book will serve as a connecting link. The Resources section contains a listing of organizations and periodicals that can help you in locating others of like mind.

You also need a way to locate sisters (and brothers) near enough to work with you closely, to cooperate in changemaking in your immediate surroundings. Here are some ways to do that.

FORM A STUDY GROUP

Women, for some reason, love to study things *en masse*. I think we are basically lonely for one another's company. And that is the big reason we congregate for one thing and another. You can form a study group on any subject you like. No matter where you begin, you can use the group to select people who might like to study changemaking with you and implement your conclusions and objectives. Bible study classes on women and the Bible, the Book of Ephesians, teaching methods, and the Church all have potential for discovering kindred souls—who may also know a kindred soul or two that you haven't come across yourself.

Eventually you can form another study group with these women. And focus your attention on whatever part of the issue of full participation of women in the Church that appeals to you most at the time.

ASK AROUND

Women hesitate to ask questions, for good reason. We know what happened to the cat who was curious. We don't want to be embarrassed, warned, avoided, or talked about. But if you ask about area women who are interested in feminist concerns, follow up leads, find out what is happening in other churches, discover if there are any women in higher levels of participation in any of them, you can often find a few women who are also feeling alone and wondering about the same things you are.

CONTACT ORGANIZATIONS FOR UNAFFILIATED PEOPLE IN YOUR AREA

Organizations working for equality for women in the Church often know of interested women in areas where there has not been enough interest yet to establish a local chapter. Such organizations can sometimes search them out for you and give you their addresses. Or they can publish your request for contacts in their newsletter.

WRITE LETTERS

Even if you cannot, or would rather not, search out kindred souls in your immediate vicinity, you can write to people who can give you moral support, advice, and assistance with information gathering and problem solving. Write to authors of articles you read whom you agree with (or disagree with but find thought provoking). Officers in organizations are usually listed somewhere on the material sent out in response to inquiries about membership. Letters to the editors can bring you information from the periodical itself and from other readers as well.

SHARING HISTORIES

One of the practices of the women's movement in general that I found interesting but did not see the point of immediately was "telling our stories." I wondered why women needed to get together and tell about their own past and struggles as a necessary part of the process of becoming whole and enlightened. I think I understand now. We each have a whole history that no one else knows. A few generations ago this would not have been true for most women. Their histories would have been known to the women in their families and their communities. Their world was smaller. They worked together. Secrets, good and bad, would have been few.

Being unknown means being alone. We need to share our stories for our own sakes. But more, we also need to share our stories for the sakes of our sisters. They will know that though they are unique, they are not unusual or strange. We all have stories to tell, and the stories bind us together again as women. Women working together, sharing, supporting one another just by knowing and understanding.

Published accounts of other women's journeys, as in Virginia Hearn's *Our Struggle to Serve* and in the accounts published in *Daughters of Sarah* and various other newsletters, are helpful to each one who reads them. Sharing our stories is one way to help us learn to work together again, beginning at the beginning, recognizing a bond. It is a way to create community, though we are separated by many miles.

LEARNING TO WORK TOGETHER AGAIN

It is too easy for women to see each other primarily as rivals. We have all been taught, through the practicalities of this world, that our allegiance to a man is what provides us with respectability and security. And not only our's but our children's respectability and security as well. Without the counterbalancing daily work together, this view of other women as possible rivals overinfluences our attitudes toward each other. Nothing stands in its way to counteract it.

So, in learning to work together again we must realize there is a long-standing natural hesitance to do so. Women often say they don't like working with other women. Such statements have been interpreted as a self-hatred of their own gender. But I suspect that is not the cause. It may be only a lack of skill in working together, coupled with natural suspicions toward potential rivals.

NEEDS WE CAN MEET TOGETHER

THE NEED FOR COMMUNITY

There is a great difference between community and exclusivism. I have repeatedly been uncomfortable in groups of women practicing exclusivism. Their way of feeling they belong is to keep someone else out. The way they know to feel good is to help someone else feel bad. Unfortunately many women (and men too) mistake the pseudo-satisfaction of exclusivity for the genuine satisfaction of community.

Community is a natural gathering of folk with commonality of purpose or experience, sharing from who they are, not from who they are pretending to be. They freely allow individuality and spontaneity.

We need community. Everybody does. That sense of community is part of the good feeling children get when they discover a place to build a fort or hideout, and work feverishly for hours or days to construct it from whatever materials they can scavenge. It is the working together for a common goal that is so satisfying. But community that deteriorates into exclusivism is not satisfying. That's what happens when the fort builders say to other children, "It's *our* fort. And YOU can't play in it!"

Within a community, we can offer and receive emotional support. What all those women who wrote me were wanting was essentially the emotional support of community, even if only a community of two members. I think though that they must have felt I had contact with others of like mind, so they would be connected indirectly to them through me. And it is true. This book is a means for making it even more true.

There is a difference between genuine emotional support and counterfeit emotional support. One way to give genuine emotional support is to make no assumptions about the other person's feelings, motivations, or actions. The way to make no assumptions is to ask, instead of guess. I do not mean pry. But if you suspect they are hurting, afraid, lonely, or overworked, rather than make assumptions about what would be supportive and act on them—ask, as graciously and nonintrusively as possible.

An aquaintance once completely and effectively blocked me from my efforts to investigate buying a house as a personal investment because she believed it would be too much work for me to restore and refurbish it myself. "For my own good" she refused to give me vital information I could get nowhere else. She seemed satisfied that she had done me a good and supportive deed. But she had made assumptions about me and my abilities, interests, work, and resources that she did not attempt to check for accuracy. That was not true emotional support.

Community demands a respect for the individual integrity and personal choice of its members. It is not necessary for us to all be the same, or to be perfectly understood, or even perfectly comfortable with each other to have community and its benefits. We can enjoy what we can, and let the rest go by. Each one is responsible for only him- or herself. We can support other people in *their own* perceptions of what their job is and what their choices ought to be.

We can offer prayer support. I remember, years ago, attending a day-long seminar for women where we learned how to use a file card box to rotate prayer requests daily—so they would all be covered systematically. I believe there was even a system for how to approach God with them. It seemed very efficient, but not something I would do while speaking with a friend. And I think of God primarily that way, as my friend.

I don't totally understand prayer, though I don't suppose that it is important that I do. But I do know that there have been times when I *knew* I was being prayed for. And was tremendously glad for it. The people praying for me at those times didn't have me on a file card I suspect. They had me on their hearts and in their thoughts. I think that is the kind of prayer support we can give each other. We can pray for each other when we care enough to remember. Not remedial praying, to make someone else more acceptable to our own personal taste, or dry systematic recitations by rote, but telling our Friend what we want for each other that respects the individuality and uniqueness we each possess.

THE NEED FOR PEERS

Although having community and having peers are similar, they are also different. I can be in community because of a common aim and still feel I have no peers, no one there very much like me.

We need to be able to find others who are like us, who understand, who share our past experiences and our hopes for the future. We need to be with those who will not need to have certain things explained. Or those who can understand our explanation because of our commonality of experience, where others would like to understand, but their experience has no parallel to make understanding really possible.

As a feminist, I need peers. And I need peers among those feminists who not only believe in equality for women but equality within a body of believers. There is a certain feeling of relief among one's peers like that felt on foreign soil when one's fellow countrywomen or countrymen appear. Ah, yes! my own kind. I think it is the relief of not having to explain oneself or a part of one's belief or actions to these people. It is a feeling of security and safety, but of exhilaration too, of discovery that one is not so strange after all. This person is similar in this way and he or she looks OK—I must be OK too.

SHARING RESOURCES AND INFORMATION

If each person had to discover the wheel for him- or herself many of us would still be walking. If all information had to be passed on by word of mouth, almost all of us would know a great deal less than we do. The reason we have universities, cities, hospitals, libraries, and many other things like government and religion is that we are willing, even eager, to share resources and information with each other. We women need to learn to share our resources and information with each other more efficiently and more widely.

In the days when women worked together, before the Industrial Revolution, they learned trades and skills from other women—mothers, aunts, grandmothers, sisters. Sharing information and resources with each other was natural, they did it as a matter of course. For us it is not so natural. We have been educated along more general lines, often taught material we would not be freely allowed to use. Girls and boys are generally taught the same material in school. There is an assumption there, that we do not particularly need to share along gender lines.

But we need to find ways to share information and resources with each other that will help make our individual and collective experiences more pleasing and satisfying. We need to pool our resources and information to get what we want for ourselves, individually and together.

MUTUAL EDIFICATION

One of the problems women have is that of believing that they must fit within any established structure. They tend to feel that they must work to be admitted *into* the hierarchical structures in the Church before they can fully share spiritually with each other. But we do not need "official" approval or position to do that.

Women can gather together in groups of from two on up to share spiritual food and learn from each other. We can engage in mutual edification. We can receive, we can give, we can share. And we can purposely arrange to do so together.

LIVING IN THE REAL WORLD

I didn't know what to call this section. I thought about calling it "Problems," or "The Flip Side," or "Thorns Among The Roses." Although I don't know exactly what to call it, I know it does need to be here because we need to learn to work together and share, fully aware that it will not all be pleasant or comfortable. Sometimes we will not get along very well. Some of us are encumbered with ways that collide with other people's ways. Sometimes people get hurt.

Shortly after my husband was fired from his job at Moody Bible Institute and events and possibilities seemed to be swirling all around me, I called a national feminist organization to ask for help with my legal possibilities. I needed advice about whether or not I should sue the religious broadcaster who had libeled and slandered me. I knew the organization had a legal department that helped women in sexual discrimination cases. As a member of that organization, I assumed that part of my dues went to support that department. But when I called on the phone, feeling very vulnerable and shaken, I was greeted by a brusque voice. My fellow feminist wasn't interested in talking with me for even a few seconds. "Put it in a letter," she said icily, and dismissed me. I never put it in a letter. I eventually let my membership lapse— and I know the treatment I received was part of the reason. I didn't feel like I belonged with people who operated that way.

Women within feminist groups have been known to savage and trash each other. Besides bringing pain and discouragement to the victims, that sort of thing also damages the work they are trying to do together. Why does it happen? And further, why work with other people if you may be making yourself vulnerable to viciousness and meanness?

Some of it comes from personal inclinations of the woman doing the savaging. She hurts, and she learned a long time ago to pass it on to the person who was most vulnerable at the moment. Or she learned to try to dethrone the king or queen. So whenever anyone seems to be succeeding or has something she would like, her automatic impulse is to tear it down. Such women exist. And some of them are among us. So I want you to know it isn't all nice and comfortable meeting needs together. You also have to watch out for falling rocks. And some of them you may not see in time to avoid.

Other problems arise from conflicting ideas about how to get things done, about what is proper bahavior, or who is in charge (or if anyone really has to be in charge), and about what is your very own business and nobody else's. It helps to stop and remember that we often come from exceedingly different backgrounds. Talkativeness may mean one thing in the South, maybe something else in the North. Courtesy and rudeness have different meanings in different places and among different ethnic and geographical groups. So while watching out for falling rocks, also be aware that some of them may only *look* like rocks. Check them to see what they are actually made of.

If you have been hit and hurt, please step back and make sure you do not make connections that would be inaccurate. If it is a personality problem, don't confuse it with an ideological difference. One disadvantage does not necessarily destroy the whole alliance.

We can learn to work together well and comfortably. Some of that will have to come from practice. And practice involves learning by making mistakes. So I hope we can pick ourselves up, dust ourselves off, and try again—making the adjustment we just learned was necessary. And continue meeting needs together.

4. Stress in Relationship

When I began speaking about equality for women in the Church to seminary and college groups, most of the people who asked questions at the end of the lecture were men. The Number One question in frequency, usually the first one, was "How does this affect marriage?"

But when I spoke to groups made up predominantly of women, the Number One question, asked with longing but almost zero expectation, was *"Are* there *any* men out there who can relate to a woman as an equal?" My answer was (and is) yes. Not too many, maybe, but more and more all the time.

Men are on the way, in process, stumbling along, *trying* to understand what in the world has happened to the women in their lives. Some of the men have arrived, sort of. Some of them may have really arrived. I don't know for sure because you can't tell for sure until you get them home. I know from reliable sources, as they say, that certain admirable public male feminists have trouble putting it into practice in their own personal relationships.

Lest you think these men are phonies, be aware that it is much harder for them to make all the belief-sorting connections with feminism than it is for women. I suspect we aren't doing too well at this either when I see in the classified section of a feminist magazine an ad for t-shirts and other paraphernalia that say, "Adam was a rough draft" and "When God made man, she was only joking." What's sexist material like this doing in a magazine that is antisexist in purpose? I haven't written to ask them how they can carry those ads. (I should have long ago, evidence that I'm not doing so well myself in the antisexism department.) But I suspect that if I did someone would say they are only harmless jokes. Not very funny to my sons and husband, who support equal rights for women, or to other men who read the magazine.

The problem is that when many changes are being made, resorting must be done on a grand scale. Belief systems are not held in isolation from each other. Whatever you believe about anything intersects with what you believe about almost everything else. So to say that it is a simple matter of treating women like whole human beings isn't so simple after all. It takes time, and a lot of stumbling around making mistakes, many of them innocent ones.

So, yes, there are men out there who want relationships with fully human women, men who are willing, even eager, to share responsibilities and opportunities with their sisters. But these men are in different stages of enlightenment and sorting of their belief systems. They make mistakes—as we do. We are going to have to teach them, gently I hope, how to treat us the way we'd like to be treated.

And then there are the other ones. Ah, yes, the sexist pigs we married, or, for some reason we can't quite fathom, are in love with, care about, admire. What about these men? How do you come to terms with a person like that? And the relatives, bosses, friends, in-laws, whom you used to like but now you aren't so sure—people who suspect you of being wrong, dangerous, outrageous, sinful, or maybe just a little crazy. How can you talk to them, keep their friendship, get along, or just maintain your cool?

HOW TO DO IT

The first rule is, don't bring up the subject at all. I know this is hard, but usually it isn't going to do anything constructive. If you must, *then only ask questions.* And only ask questions in the gentlest of manners and in the most unexplosive of situations.

For example, your mother-in-law remarks about your young son, "My, he's certainly *all boy,* isn't he!" This may be more than your self-control can safely ignore. You feel you must say *something* in response. The temptation will probably be to lecture on nonsexist childrearing and give a brief history of the feminist movement and its aims in the next several years, including your own work in your area of interest.

The result will be that this innocent grandmother who was trying, in her own way, however flawed, to admire her grandson, your son, is going to be challenged and possibly taken to task. If you realize that her statement doesn't mean the same thing to you as it does to her, you can ask yourself if anything is to be served by saying anything at all. If the answer is yes, you might try asking a question like "Hmm, what do you mean?" (Incidentally, a very profitable and worthwhile question in almost any tight place.) Then if she replies that he is active and outgoing, or something of the sort, you can say, "Yes, Liza (your daughter) is like that too, I'm so glad they are both outgoing children." Or, "Yes, I like children to be able to be free and lively. I hope any children I might have would be that way."

This reply releases pressure in you and gently and unobtrusively re-educates her by taking behavior out of a sex-specific category and applying it to both genders.

What if the conversation does not end there? Let's say she makes a negative statement about the subject dear to your heart, equality for women. In that case, either ask another information-gathering question ("What do you mean?") and/or *make a statement from your experience.* Tell only what you have felt, heard, seen, and thought. It is difficult to debunk someone else's own experience without appearing rude. I know that will not stop some people. They will say, "Well, you are wrong!" Or "You are mistaken!" If that is their response, remain silent. It is unproductive to argue with closed minds and defensive people. Let the subject drop exactly there. Actually, it is a potential advantage to you to do so if they have been obviously rude to you. They will be uncomfortable (we hope they have some sense of decency) and possibly apologize or say something later in a milder tone. In that case,

1. Ask information gathering questions.
2. Find areas of agreement between you. People can usually agree on a larger issue. Keep looking until you find one.
3. Share from your own experience.
4. *When* it is asked for, share information from an observer-searcher position ("I wondered about x so I searched and I found . . .").

This way, any dispute is not with you personally, but with the information, its source, the writer, etc. You can thus depersonalize any disagreement about the issue. That will make it easier for the other person to think about the subject area more openly than if the personal element is attached to it.

THE BIBLICAL PRINCIPLE OF MUTUAL SUBMISSION

Before I go further, I would like to present an overiding principle that applies to all relationships and that I think is extremely helpful in dealing with the stress-in-relationship that results from differences of opinion or understanding on the issue of equality. The discovery of this principle was a bonus from the research for my book *Heirs Together,* which is about equality in marriage. I was checking the context and original language of a passage in Ephesians chapter 5 that is traditionally used to restrict women and place them firmly under their husbands' control. I found that the passage teaches, instead, a principle of mutuality.

The first phrase of Ephesians 5:22 is usually translated, "Wives, submit to your husbands," a command. Actually, it says nothing of the sort. In the original Greek, it says, "Wives, to your husbands," with no command at all. The phrase, which in most English translations begins a new paragraph, sometimes even a new section, is actually a continuation of the previous verse, which says "Submitting yourselves to one another in the fear of Christ . . ." The only command in the passage is back in Verse 18, which says, "Be filled with the Spirit."[4]

The principle of mutual submission, a sort of voluntary raising everyone else to your own personal level of importance and worthiness, was a way to unify a diverse mixture of social levels and relations into a mutually satisfying and mutually edifying body, the Church. This equalizing principle works well in all relationships, and can be implemented in any social structure—because it involves the superseding of social divisions by a mutual valuing of one another.

It gives others the freedom to be who they are without intrusion. It also gives you the freedom to be who you are without intrusion. Each of you is able to say, in effect, "I will not lord it over you, and by the same token I will not let you lord it over me, either."

If you apply this principle to the relationships that are stressed because of new awareness on your part concerning equality for women, you will find, I think, a doorway into destressing those relationships to a considerable degree. If you apply this principle, you will of necessity do several things:

GIVE OTHERS THE OPTION TO NOT CHANGE

I know this is hard to do, but if we are to be free *to* change, others must also be free to *not* change. That is not to say they won't change. They probably will, to some extent, whether they want to or not, purely because of the ways their behavior is entwined with ours. But they must have freedom of choice if true change, positive and general, is to come about. This means you must give them the honest choice of disagreeing with you and remaining convinced of what they now believe. To do otherwise is to intrude on their own persons, doing violence to their minds and belief systems, taking a freedom from them that we do not want taken from us.

So, hard as it is, I believe we must approach those in relationships with us with a commitment to dealing with them kindly and honorably even if they stay the absolute same.

GIVE OTHERS ROOM TO CHANGE

After allowing for the possibility, the *all-right* possibility that the other person may not change at all his or her views about women and equality, we then deal with allowing the other person the space he or she needs to change, *if and when he or she wants to.*

I have tried to limit my discussions of equality for women to people who want to talk about it, never pursuing further than they want to go. I expected that many people would not agree with me. And I was certainly right about that. Some were vehemently opposed and emphatically said so. One man wrote a letter, heartily disagreeing with me, to the editor of a magazine in which I had published an article. I didn't know him, but knew someone who did. My acquaintance assured me the letter writer was absolutely firm in his opposition to equal participation for women. I really did not expect this man to change. I wouldn't have even tried to convince him of my view if I had had the chance.

But somehow he read a copy of my book *Woman Be Free,* a biblical apologetic for women's equality in the Church. And a few years later our mutual acquaintance told me the man came to him and said he had totally changed his mind on the subject. He was now in favor of equality for women. Every so often I hear of a similar turnaround, a complete reversal. I think these people change because they have the room to think it over for themselves. I purposefully wrote the book in such a way as to present information in a noncoercive manner. I suspect that the woman in his life, who also wanted him to change, discussed the issue noncoercively with him as well.

As long as people have pressure on them to change their minds, they have something to defend—their own mental processes, their inner integrity. But if there is no need to defend their position because no one is pushing them into a corner, they are free to be curious and to think it over for themselves.

One woman, whose husband was a teacher, for years discussed equality for women with him in long evening talks. He held to his belief that women should not become pastors, even after he eventually conceded that all other claims for equality were valid. She was surprised when one day he said, "I think I should admit that I have been teaching your views for years. I am now convinced." The man had shifted his opinion so gradually that he was not completely aware that he agreed. The final area of disagreement had fallen through his reading in an unrelated area. But he had waited a long time before telling her. Why, I don't know. Maybe he needed time to make the change his own.

When I began work on my first book, some of my husband's students knew about what I was doing and sometimes used me as a study resource when working on a related subject. In one such situation, a group of six students came out to the suburbs one evening to interview me for a class presentation on the issue of equality for women as it applied to a New Testament passage they were studying. The group consisted of five women and one man. It happened that the women were taking the positive side of the issue, women could participate equally with men. The man took the negative position, that they should not.

I should point out that these were Moody Bible Institute students, who tend to be of high caliber in every way, intelligent, courteous, and thoughtful. And these were no different—not, that is, until the man began asking questions in a way that appeared increasingly doltish to the young women. They could not understand why he continued in his innocent and ignorant delusions that women should be quiet and work in the church nursery and little else. They became angry with him and began to verbally attack him. I became his defender, eventually almost his physical defender. They were not at all willing for him to remain oblivious to what seemed so obvious a truth to them. They demanded he change there and then before their eyes. I insisted that he be given room to continue as he was until such time as he himself saw things differently, if that ever came. I defended his right to be respected and treated courteously even if he was going to be a traditionalist.

It's really hard for many women to not take it personally when a man smiles and says things that would restrict their own personal lives and the lives of all women. They take it personally because it is personal, to them. But it isn't to him. He doesn't experience your reality. Neither does he perceive the implications for you of what he has said. He is so accustomed to thinking as he does that to continue to do so seems utterly logical and reasonable. The conviction long ago that the earth was flat or that the sun revolved around a stationary earth took time and observation to change. Views we grew up with, especially those that do not affect us, never have, and we think never will, change slowly.

THE TIME ELEMENT IN CHANGING BELIEF SYSTEMS

The reason the men in our lives can't just trot out their logical minds and accept the reasonableness of our overwhelming proofs and agree with us at once has to do with the nature of belief systems. Evangelists from my childhood used to say they did not want to pick fruit green. At least the more responsible ones didn't want to. They meant they did not want to have people become Christians as a result of a high-pressure sales job and return the merchandise tomorrow, or never use it, leaving it on the shelf of their lives as an embarrassingly poor buying experience. We have to allow the people we care about time to make the mental connections and shifts necessary for their own comfortable decisions.

REMEMBER WHAT YOU SHARE

When a subject has the power that equality (or the lack of it) has, it can supersede all other issues and subjects we had in common before it arrived. That is the problem with most stressed relationships. We find it hard to focus on the good because the bad hurts so much. But equality for women, equal opportunity, equal personhood is something we have been given by God, something we take for ourselves. It is not something we must get from some other human being. We are only dealing with thought patterns. The rest we can change by working for it. But the relationships we want to keep and nourish must be allowed to have a freedom that goes beyond that one issue. We need to remember what we share with those we care about, rather than focusing on what we differ about. I didn't say *ignore,* just not focus on it.

And we do share a great deal, or we wouldn't be in the relationship in the first place. The agenda for change is a separate agenda from much we can talk about and do together. It helps to remember that and act upon it. One way to do that is *to actually be doing something* about that agenda in a meaningful and satisfying way. It allows us the space to do something else and think about something else the rest of the time.

THE TONGUE OF THE WISE HEALS

Try putting your concerns and requests in a positive frame *every time* you talk to the person with whom you are in a stressful relationship. It's an interesting experiment, anyway, to listen to yourself for a couple of days and see how many times you frame things positively and how many negatively. Some people hardly talk any other way than negatively. They say, "Not bad," when you ask, "How are you?" They say, "Don't forget," when they want you to remember, "Be sure and *don't* do that," when they mean they want you to be sure and *do* something else.

Watch your speech for a while and experiment with *how* you are saying what you want (or what you don't want). See if you can translate everything that you are inclined to put in a negative frame into a positive one.

Avoid the accusations that come to your lips. See if you can say it in a way that does not impute motive and malice to what may be only acting the way he or she has all along before *you* became sensitized to it. Sexist remarks are *no worse* after we become aware of how damaging and wrong they are. Thus those using them are *no more guilty* than they were before we knew to be offended.

BEING TRUE TO YOURSELF TWENTY-FOUR HOURS A DAY

Lest you think I am Pollyanna in a wishy-washy dress, I want to let you know that all of the above will get you nowhere fast if you are not at the same time true to yourself and the enlightenment and convictions you have twenty-four hours a day. It is possible to be *nice* and *strong* at the same time. It isn't real easy, especially at first. We have all the wrong socialization for doing this in relationships. But if you will borrow from another area of your life and experience you can do it quite well. You probably already are able to be nice *and* strong too with children, maybe also with pets. I have seen some really nice strength used by small women on large horses. If the child isn't going to have his medicine and you know he has to, you are quite good at this nice strength.

And there is firm strength. Not mean, not angry, not accusative, just firm and immovable. That will be necessary some of the time. Maybe not often, but you need it in your repertoire.

When you determine who you are, a whole person, a fully human person, and what you want—treatment and opportunity compatible with that full humanity—then you, in order to be true to yourself, operate with that in mind. Things that used to be tolerated can be quietly not tolerated.

I know what will happen if your behavior begins to reflect being true to yourself twenty-four hours a day—both nothing and a whole lot. Some situations will prompt absolutely no response at all. It wasn't even necessary for you to do some of what you did all those years, and you didn't know it. Other responses will be shock. I still remember the look on the woman's face when I, as a young pastor's wife, finally took my own life in hand and said no, I wouldn't be at a certain women's meeting. But, like her, many in your life will quickly become accustomed to your new independence.

Another response will be outrage at your supposed inconsideration, foolishness, selfishness, inefficiency, whatever. Those respondents too will adjust if you maintain your commitment to your own personhood without fuss. Then there is the humor response, the "Isn't she funny? *Oh, my!*" Ignoring that works very well.

But then there is the vicious response. Some women will receive a fist in the mouth for treating themselves like whole people, either a real fist or a figurative one. You know who you are. And I am saying that that is not being true to yourself, to walk into a fist. When you are dealing with someone like that, then you need something much more than confrontation, either direct or indirect. You need protection and escape. You have an agenda that supersedes equality for women in the Church—it's survival, either physical or emotional, or both. Being true to yourself here is getting help, getting away, getting a better relationship or none at all.

WHEN A RELATIONSHIP DETERIORATES

One of the things that happens to some women is that being true to themselves in the form of claiming their equality brings about a lot more trouble at home. They are tempted to wonder if *they* are somehow at fault. It is *possible* to go about changemaking in such a way as to cause trouble. But a more common reason is that the relationship was in trouble before. Added stress only made the underlying problem more obvious.

ABUSIVE RELATIONSHIPS

Many abusive marriages are maintained through the long-suffering and tolerance of the wife. When she becomes no longer willing to tolerate, marriage problems may seem worse. A woman who is no longer willing to be abused will receive increased attempts at abuse in an effort to maintain control over her. In the case of verbal and emotional abuse, it may involve long argumentation to the effect that she is causing problems, that things used to be so fine before she changed. Which is true, but only for the abuser.

You need to know that your feminist ideas and any resulting changes in your actions may not be the true cause of conflict between you, even if it seems that they are. Since we, as women, have been taught to be responsible for the success or failure of relationships, we do a lot of patching and smoothing to try to maintain relationships far beyond their useful and fair life. We tend to believe it is our fault if they fail.

Oppressive or domineering spouses may seem easier to live with as long as you defer to them and live within the bounds and perimeters of *their* comfort. Whenever you, for whatever reason, move outside those perimeters their tolerance level for change will soon be exceeded and their behavior will become much worse. The cause is not your changing but their basic oppression and domination. Your changing is only the catalyst, not the cause, for their increasingly bad treatment of you and opposition to your activities and ideas.

I suspect a substantial number of women reading this book are in abusive relationships. Such women tend to be nurturing types. Selected by their men for the ability to hang in there with an immature, demanding, and destructive partner, they tend to be loyal, helpful, and tolerant. Hard-working and loving, they are the kind that rescue puppies. Such people are drawn to causes and want to help everyone have a better life. Working for a larger cause outside their own personal misery, something they feel they *can* make better, can provide a means of escape from some of the pressure.

These women have been exquisitely sensitized to oppression. They are trying to free themselves by freeing all women. This is their perception of a first step outward.

They may not change things at home because

1. They don't know they are victims of abuse. Not all abuse is as obvious as physical battering. Emotional abuse is sometimes subtle (but no less destructive) and hard to identify.
2. They feel trapped in their personal situations, feeling it will cost them or others in their families too much socially, financially, professionally, and/or emotionally to leave.

If you are one of these women or suspect you may be, let me encourage you to educate yourself about the nature of abuse. The Resources section of this book contains a list of factors present in abusive relationships to help identify them, and a list of resources available for getting help and helping yourself.

WOMEN WHO OPPOSE EQUALITY FOR WOMEN

One of the most difficult people for most of us to deal with is the woman who adamantly and vociferously opposes what we are trying to do for all of us. It may be ironic and even funny to hear a woman loudly demanding her right to remain silent in the Church, but it hurts and puzzles us. Why are these women doing this? And why are they so intense? Some seem fanatical and frantic in their desperation to keep on being submitted, silent, and unequal.

Years ago, when I was a pastor's wife, I accompanied my husband on a pastoral call to a very strict and conservative family. Since none of the churches in the area could meet their strict requirements, they conducted their own services at home. I do not remember who brought up the issue of women's participation during our visit. I don't think it was me because that was years before I did much more than ask questions from time to time about certain Bible passages. But the woman of the house, the wife and mother of the clan, thrust her Bible at us, and tapping it vigorously with a finger, emphatically warned us about the evils and dangers of women not being properly submissive and silent. I was struck then, as I have been many times since, with the incongruity of a woman loudly doing what she says women are not to do.

I went away from that visit thinking about why, why did it mean so much to her? It didn't seem strange to me that women would hold such views. I had attended a series of conservative, fundamentalist churches. I knew what was taught and believed. What I couldn't understand was why she held her view with such intensity. I finally decided it was possibly because the woman had given up a tremendous amount of herself, her opportunities and inclinations, to conform to this teaching. If the teaching turned out to not be true, then she had given up everything for nothing. It would be a total loss to her, an unnecessary loss, a great robbery. And that would be too much to bear. So she held her bad bargain even more tightly lest it be revealed as less than perfect and not God's only choice for her. Since that time, I think I have always seen evidence of that fear underneath the outward façades of women who go to great lengths to oppose equality for us. I've seen angry façades, saccharine sweet façades, and icy cold ones. But I suspect fear is behind all of them, fear for what they have lost, if it turns out they have lost it unnecessarily.

I treat such women kindly. They are not my enemies. They may *act* like enemies, so I am careful about them. But I do not suppose that they are people I need to hate or disdain.

I'm not very comfortable about run-ins with them, though. Just last week I received the second phone call from one who was genteel and courteous. She had noticed, in the introductory chapter of my book *The Complete Woman,* a list of manipulative, traditionalist books that tell women how to be less. These were books I was writing to expose, to oppose, to reveal for what they are, misusers of women, false advisors. But, she said, she had read one and just loved it, so she went and read another one and loved it too. Her problem was she couldn't locate the third one. Did I know where she could get a copy? No, actually I didn't. But, kind person that I was trying to be, I told her the name of the publisher, author, and date of publication.

That first call was months ago. Last week she called again. Did I want to sell her my copy of the hard-to-find book by any chance, since it was now out of print? No, I didn't—for several reasons, all of which you can probably guess. But again, I was courteous and helpful. I said sometime she might like to read my first book, which gives biblical evidence for the other side of the issue. No, she said, she wouldn't be interested because she *knew* the Bible commanded women to submit to their husbands and she loved it that way.

But she was just a little too breathless and hurried in her claims of delight. I thought I heard the note of fear underneath. So I went away from the phone with mixed feelings, uncomfortable ones. I had the feeling I was helping someone into further darkness while trying to pull her out, even though I didn't send her the book. I always feel that way in such an interchange. I try to not preach or impose my views. I share if they listen; if they won't, I stop. I always hope that I have left the door open for them so that someday, if they want to know more, they will feel welcome and come back. I don't know anything more to do. I wish I did, because I know they are my sisters too. And they are afraid.

A few women who take the traditional position ride it into personal political power. I do not know any of them personally so I can't say why they do what they do. I suspect it is not from fear, but from political savvy, a knowledge of leverage and group psychology. I don't know. But I watch out for them, they have sharp teeth. I recommend that you do the same.

UNCOMFORTABLE FEMINISTS

Feminists come in all shapes and sizes, and all psychological hues. Feminism makes strange traveling companions sometimes. We are not all smooth and soothing personalities. Some of us are porcupine-like, pricking everyone who gets into the wrong position in our presence. Some of us are just a mite weird, usually in an endearing way, but not always. But many of us are ordinary, plain, usual, and compatible people. We are diverse.

We are different, not because we are feminists, but because we are people. But because women who are unusual, prickly, and just a mite weird are double outcasts, they make very intense feminists, willing to work hard and long for the cause. Being free, equal, and opportunitied means more to them than it does to the multitudes of ordinary women who have been less discriminated against in every setting. Because of this you might find a higher incidence of the "uncomfortable" feminist in the working ranks of some organizations. I can't prove this, but I suspect it is true. Even there they are in the minority, but they can be found. So some people complain that feminists are abrasive, or eccentric, or unusual, not representative of other women. Well, that's not true, they are representative of women's beliefs about equality. Their personal preferences and personalities are their own. We don't need to confuse the two.

I think such women add color and dimension to the movement and I am glad they are there. But when someone says that so-and-so is hard to get along with and insults people, implying it is her feminist views that are at the base of it, I am careful to point out the obvious angels among us. And then I go into my spiel about unusual women being doubly discriminated against.

We also need to be aware of the practice of discounting anything we want as women that the traditionalists do not want to allow by claiming that those who want or need it are "exceptions." This might be called Playing Exception. It is done to blacks, children, old people, to anyone who is a disadvantaged minority and wants a fair deal or human treatment. It goes like this: Bob and Bill are executives, complaining about working wives and mothers, about how unfair and unreasonable it is for women to abdicate their positions at home and work elsewhere. Their co-worker Mary overhears the conversation and says, "Joan and I are working wives and mothers." Bill replies, "Oh, you're different," and drops the subject. Neither man is aware of the incongruity and absurdity of their logic.

When feminists introduce issues, pursue goals, and present relevant information they are often dismissed by someone Playing Exception: "Oh, she's just a frustrated old maid." Or, "She just needs a good lay." "She probably can't get along with her own husband." "She is just a castrating bitch." The implication is that the woman wanting something they don't want her to have is *out of place,* thus not a *real* woman, thus dismissable. We need to make sure this game isn't successfully used against any of us who happen to be personally a little different. We need to know when we are actually doing something that is counterproductive and when we are only having Playing Exception used on us.

5. Crisis in Faith

This is my second attempt to write to you. . . . There is so much frustration in me that it will not be sorted out to neat lines on paper. . . . Churches sure muck everything up.

I've become more and more detached from church—spiritually and mentally as the process of growth-life has gone along. Without fail I repreach each sermon I hear. Not only are these sermons slanted by a male hierarchy, but worse yet there seems to be a general lack of truth and consistency. I can never figure out how people are called to preach, yet seem so incapable of spreading out the word of God before us and inviting us to come and partake of the feast. . . . As long as I can remember I've rebelled inwardly, not knowing why until recent years.

. . . it is often hard, when working within the restrictions . . . to remember that I am not less, to keep reminding myself that I have my own intellectual responsibility before God. Let's face it—as a general rule women are not seen as intellectual beings within the church.

But still I thought the issue was not for me to think about and discuss. And I have stayed on the fringes for years, vaguely guilt-ridden, unresolved, uncomprehending of what the issues really are, thinking perhaps everyone around me was right and I was the odd one out, but unwilling to make the compromise even if I was wrong.

I have always felt a bit of an outcast or "unspiritual" when I have tried to stand for the freedoms I believe Christ died to give *all* regardless of their sex.

If my "being" was as worthless as I was led to believe, then what did I have to live for. And if the Bible said what the Christian community that I knew said it did, then I would have to look elsewhere for my "meaning for living."

It never sat right, although for a time I said I believed it because "one couldn't be a true Christian if one didn't." (I knew I was a Christian, ergo . . .) . . . I still couldn't believe I was limited because of my gender. (You mean women *never* have a gift of teaching?) And the people I was arguing with were seminarians who would tell me the Greek supported them. But I felt like I didn't know if I even wanted a part of that God that punished me for being female (it wasn't *my* fault). But I never left the faith—just ceased discussing the issues surrounding women.

I had an extremely difficult childhood, and have spent the last couple of years learning to love myself and accept myself as a special person in God's eyes, capable of doing and being anything, and getting ready to soar to the mountaintops because I was a free person—free to be what God had originally created me to be. Then, all of a sudden, smash—I was nothing again.

I have put a lot of things on hold this past month; first, my relationship with God. I had to stop reading parts of the Bible because all it talked about was the rebellious people of God, and I was just falling deeper and deeper into condemnation. Second, my relationship with the body here that we are committed to. We have a fairly open worship service, and I had gotten over my fear of starting songs and reading scriptures out loud. Now I have no desire to participate in the worship service. I feel like my contribution is unwanted. . . . I guess my biggest problem is that I feel so alone. I have no one to talk to now and I am afraid to move in any direction. Sometimes I feel like "they" are right and I am going to be severely punished for my rebellion. Most of the time I just try not to think about it at all, because it's such a source of misery.

I sometimes wonder how people can believe in a God who gives women talents and capacities equal to those of men, and then says not to use them, on account of their sex. It makes no sense at all.

Women are breaking on the rocks of traditionalism in our churches. Wherever I go, whenever I write on the subject of equality for women, or am interviewed in print, they reach out and tell me their stories. They write me letters, not necessarily for help, often just to have *someone* to tell, to have some outlet for the inner pressure, pain, and disappointment.

I have quoted so many women here in order to make it clear that I am not talking about a small problem held in isolation by a few women sprinkled around the country in only a few churches. The crisis of faith brought about by the savaging of women in their churches reaches everywhere and affects many, many women. When you consider that I am only one writer, that I am not someone to whom great numbers of people have access, and that the proportion of people with a problem to those who actually write a letter about it is large, the true scope of the problem becomes apparent. Women sensitized to the issue of equality for women in the Church are experiencing a crisis of faith everywhere.

HOW IT HAPPENS

The traditional teaching of the Church regarding women requires two things of them. First, that they suspend disbelief when faced with evidence that is contradictory to the restrictive practices and beliefs of the traditionalist position. Second, that women disregard their own perceptions whenever those perceptions conflict with the traditionalist belief system. Whenever a woman reads passages of Scripture that do not square with the restrictive position, she must suspend her disbelief of the system and allow a mental glitch in her reasoning to occur. The glitch remains to join other glitches that accumulate over time. The same thing happens when an unfair practice occurs and an "explanation" is given.

Whenever a woman perceives unfairness and inconsistency in the traditionalist restrictions, she is required to disregard her own perceptions. These two processes of inner violation contribute to a growing sense of not being able to trust one's own self, of being inner-unreliable, of not being competent to make value judgments. It also contributes to a sense of losing one's own self, of not being able to lay claim to one's own thought processes and trust them. Other people must be relied upon to define one's self, to determine perimeters of personal behavior and thought.

Over time, this denouncing of one's own self and personal integrity causes an intense stress point where it intersects with honesty and personal responsibility. Sitting in the church, the woman is told that God holds her personally responsible, while, at the same time, she is not allowed to be.

In an effort to solve her dilemma, she *thinks about* the different forces pulling against each other, trying to sort them out. They will not sort. She then *looks for more information.* This leads to *asking questions* of those who she has trusted to tell her the truth—the Church hierarchy. And this step often leads to reproof and warnings.

In order to maintain her sanity and some sense of personal integrity, she then goes, on her own, to look for more information. And when she finds it, she at first distrusts it precisely because she has been taught

to distrust her own inner thought processes. It appeals to her, seems true
—therefore it is suspect.

A woman who has the personal integrity and the tenacity to get this
far, who feels compelled to go to such lengths to find the truth and
satisfy her inner longing to do the right thing before God, to be true
and honest within herself, to make things make sense, is now ripe for
disaster. She will undoubtedly search further, be further convinced.
And then she will want to share her discoveries with people she hopes
will help her decide; or if she has already decided, will help her make
changes in the Church's practice.

Women who arrive at this place in their personal journeys toward
wholeness then come up against the brick wall of the power structure
that is common to all institutionalized groups. She will be hurt.

If she is afraid to share what she is wondering about, or has found
out and is convinced of, she will sit in church increasingly uncomfortable and stressed because she is forced into an outward immobility
while things are going on inside her demanding action. She wants to
do something. What, she does not know, because every avenue to doing
something, whatever it might be, is closed to her.

She hears sexist language, jokes, and illustrations. She notices that
women are invisible in sermons, lessons, and art. She notices all the
whole superstructure of sexism and restriction of her gender. And it
becomes overwhelming. Not just because it is terrible, victimizing, and
painful, but also because she can do nothing at all about it.

Women are in a pack of trouble when they get to this point. We,
taught to behave like good mothers no matter whether it involves
mothering or not, will sit in terribly stressful situations waiting for
things to get better. We do not naturally think about meeting our needs
for emotional survival and health. We think only of trying to solve
problems without disturbing the structures around us. We think if we
work hard, do our best, continue to be "good" people, change will
happen. That is the way things are supposed to work. That is the way
we have been told they will work. That is even the way they do work
in some areas of our lives. But that is not the way they work when
you come up against rigid structures of power and institutionalism. The
way they work here is that women acting like good mothers get

ground up in the gears of the institutional machine, whether it is a small one like a local church or a large one like a conglomerated college-publishing house-radio-television empire.

So we have a crisis on several levels, of personal physical-emotional survival (from the effects of stress), in relationships, and in our faith. How, in all the conflicting and changing belief systems, do we sort out and sift through what we believe about God? And all of us ask at some time in this, why did he allow things to be like this? And how could he allow *us* to be victimized? At the least we want to know if God is really our friend. Or could we have been wrong there too?

DETERMINING WHOSE FAULT IT REALLY IS

We believe in an orderly universe. It is the way we learned to think. We believe that things do make sense, at least if you discover enough facts. But it is often not possible, given our state as limited beings, to know enough facts to make sense of everything. So, for practical purposes, we cannot assume that we can detect the patterns in the orderly universe. Things sometimes can't be traced to their source. At least not by us. And that is the case with whose fault it is.

Every woman who goes along the route I have described will at some point be consumed with an overwhelming anger at what has been done to her, to other women, to the Church. She will be angry about the loss, the terrible personal loss, the lost resources to the Church. But she will not know what to do with her anger. She would like to find the person or persons responsible for this outrage and settle accounts, do justice. Anger needs an object. Otherwise it burns internally and consumes its host.

But there is no one who is responsible. If you blame the male chauvinists who savaged you personally, remember that they are acting out of behavior patterns they accepted unquestionably, that *you* probably accepted at some time in your past. They aren't hurting; they have no reason to know that the ways they are behaving are wrong. They operate out of ignorance. If you blame the theologians of the past like Thomas Aquinas (if he was so smart, why didn't he figure this one out too?), you must remember that the man was progressive for his time, but that he built his conclusions on Aristotelian thought and just figured out a way to make everything fit together. He had to round off a few things to make them fit; women were one of those things.

If you are going to blame God—and this is where the main crisis in faith occurs—recognize that if God is going to allow free will, he has to allow us the freedom to be wrong. And we will be victimized to some extent for the wrong choices of other people exercising that freedom.

If it isn't anybody's fault, and I'm convinced it isn't, what do we do with our anger? If we try to ignore it, it will eat us out inside. It will also seek victims. Then we will vent it on the convenient, the unsuspecting, and the innocent. Most of those who get burned by our anger will be male. So we, abhorring sexism, will turn it back on other people on the basis of their sex. No good or fair solution there.

What you do with your anger is, first of all, you recognize it and own it. It is a just and fair anger. There are real inequities to be angry about. It is the only reasonable response to what has happened. Your anger is something you have a right to. Second, you find something to use your anger *for* rather than someone to use it *on*.

A woman who is a nurse approached me at a church where I was speaking. She said she was full of anger about the way male doctors condescended to nurses, screwing up things for the patients, and leaving the messes to the nurses—but objected when they responded as capable professionals rather than as submissive females. She told me about a session in which the ideal nurse was portrayed as a stereotypical submissive woman. She was furious about all of it but felt unable to change the situation in any way.

I told her I wrote the first draft of my first book absolutely burning people to the ground who oppressed women. I fried them up extra crispy. Then I rewrote again and again until I could retain the fire but without singeing anybody. I shared how much better I felt when I was doing something constructive with my anger, writing a book that would help change the situation. Was there some area she could make a beginning for change in and work on that? An area she knew well, beginning where she was?

She said, yes, she could write an article for a nursing journal. When

I saw her again some time later, she told me that she had not only written the article but was at work on several other changemaking projects, some with other nurses. When she began to think in terms of using her anger as a fuel for change it lost its destructive aspects for her.

DEALING WITH RIGIDITY, DISHONESTY, CRUELTY, ABUSE, AND DISILLUSIONMENT

But anger isn't the biggest problem we face when confronted, close up, with the conflicts between traditionalism and equality. There are the wounds. What do you do when you have been savaged, ravaged, despoiled, and you don't think you will ever be the same again? How do you get over it? Do you get over it?

Within the family of faith, the Church, there is the assumption, carefully tended in many ways, that it *is* a family. This family feeling is carefully nurtured in parachurch organizations such as mission agencies, schools, and other institutions. We believe, because of what we have been taught and have experienced, that this family feeling orientation represents the true state of affairs. That's not necessarily so. At least it isn't the whole story. Another, less well known, reason for fostering the family feeling orientation in organizations is that it makes the members more controllable. It makes them less apt to ask for raises in pay, equity, and accountability. I have seen too many examples of this in action to doubt it anymore. But there was a time, before wounding, when I had the luxury of ignorance.

When a Christian college refuses to reveal its pay scales and claims it is because the administration does not want to violate the privacy of its employees, it is trading on that family feeling. When the college gives a pay raise to Professor X and tells him, "Don't tell anyone else what your raise was, because no one else got one," the administration is trading on that family feeling (don't embarrass your brother). And when the teachers are paid very poorly, the family feeling is again exploited by appealing to all members to pull together: "there is not enough money because we are trying to do a good work together for God." When obvious inequities between the workers and members of the administration are accidentally revealed, the disparity in treatment is ignored, or silenced by an appeal to family harmony, to not being divisive or stirring up trouble.

This typical misuse of the family orientation among Christians is prevalent throughout the parachurch world. For this reason, anyone within that world is vulnerable to victimization when they step outside the particular set of prohibitions of the group they are associated with.

Because of this pseudo-family orientation and its polarity, the non in-groupness of anyone who does not belong to the particular group, falling out of favor means the equivalent of being cast out into outer darkness. The effects are much worse than ordinary social ostracism. Because of the *family* orientation, offense against structural prohibitions by a woman (or anyone else) places her in the outsider category. She is a nobody, literally, out of everything that once was the family. This is part of what is behind the anguish, loneliness, and lostness evident in some of the letters I quoted from at the beginning of this chapter. The effect of being ejected from such a "family" is a profound lostness, an emotional immobility much like that of an abandoned child. But not a child just abandoned by its parents, but by its siblings, aunts, uncles, cousins, grandparents, and all.

Since so many of the offending person's beliefs about themselves and about God and their relationship to God are connected in experience to that family of faith, those beliefs are all affected by the expulsion. Even if you still go to the place where you were a part of that family, attending church, keeping the job, staying in the relationship, the expulsion is still there. You know you are out, considered a nonmember. The effects are profound and deep.

I watched the effect such treatment had on my husband, an excellent teacher, after he was fired from his job as a result of the smear campaign I mentioned earlier.

He became increasingly immobilized, lost confidence in his ability to teach, sat depressed and wondering if all was lost. In actual fact, he had lost nothing at all other than his position within a parachurch organization. If he had lost a job as a teacher in a secular college, there would have been a much less wrenching result. But because he had bought into the family belief system that was a part of his work, he was immobilized when he lost it. It had become a part of his own identity. It took months, even years, to rebuild and resort his belief systems to accommodate his new understandings about what had actually been going on all those years he had believed and acted upon being a member of "one big Christian family."

Loss of official position or rejection by the official structure is only the first wave of wounding. After the initial casting out of the family comes the peripheral disillusioning that begins just as one thinks the situation is now going to be all right. When my husband was fired, our family received a tremendous amount of support from people we knew and from those we had never met. We were encouraged and sustained by reassurances from those supporters. But within the wider circle of the "family" of believers we had associated ourselves with for years we received a progressive orphaning that was devastating.

An example of the kind of thing that would happen without any way of predicting it: a woman from our church, whom I respected and knew fairly well, asked kindly and solicitously (I thought, sincerely) how we were getting along after the firing. I told her about the good results and emotional support. She asked how our children were responding to what had happened. I then told her, with sorrow, that one of my teenage sons could no longer bear to attend church, anywhere, because of the way his father had been treated by his co-workers and the religious establishment. Her response was an immediate physical recoil, a look of disgust, and "Oh, sick!" uttered in shock. My son found himself outside the church family and refused to go. I was being orphaned from this woman's relative list at the moment. This sort of thing continues in waves as the ripples extend further from the original parting of the organizational ways.

Even now, several years later, lies told about us at that time still come back. Lies we could never trace down and counter. But they separate us permanently from the "family of insiders" in many people's minds.

TRANSITIONAL MENDING

What does one do to heal the rip caused by being cast out, severed from the insider position? One sets about healing the wounds, first of all by distancing. A book that was a great help to me in the first couple of years after my husband lost his job is *Transitions,* by William Bridges. In it the author says that every change involves a similar transition process. It doesn't matter what the change is, even a positive change we have wanted, like marrying someone we love. They all involve the same three steps. First there is a leaving behind of the old situation, state, or position. A time of loss, so to speak. Then follows an interval of disequilibrium during which we feel listless and do not know what to do. We feel disoriented and aimless. Next there is a new beginning, a stepping into the new situation and making the fine adjustments that come with new settings, situations, and associations.

Bridges says that all three stages are essential for a successful transition. If you short-change any step, the transition will be incomplete. There will be snags that plague you, discomfort that will never quite go away. He says that any stage may be longer than the others, that you must not rush them, but work through them. You must especially not try to rush the middle one, or omit it. There is a real need for the disequilibrium, gestational stage between leaving the old and beginning the new.

So the first thing you do is distance yourself. You begin the process of leaving that which is lost. You recognize that you did not know that the people who hurt you would do that, but they did. You face it in all its ugliness. If they stole from you, even your good name, they did. It was done.

Then you move beyond the old into a time of mending and resorting your priorities, your beliefs, your desires, and your understanding of yourself. I think that is the greatest benefit to be gotten from the wounds that come from such encounters, the self-learning that can take place. You often find, I think, that you have been denying your perceptions about other people and about yourself for a long time. It no longer seems to be a worthwhile thing to do. You are ready to toss all of that aside. You feel like the woman who said, "I am seventy-six years old and I no longer care what anybody thinks about me. I do what I want to."

About this stage, I should say, that it lasts longer than you think. We, several times, have remarked to each other that we thought we had recovered from what happened to us, only to find later that we had not. The mending, resorting, and healing may take a long time. But the things you now know are worth a great deal. As someone else said, experience is a great teacher, but she is rough. You may not think so for a long time, but you will be surprised to find it is true—your education is valuable.

The next stage, the new beginning, comes as the initial stage is drawing to a close. One comes to terms with the new view of reality, finds there are other people in the world, other groups to enjoy time and space with, new uses for one's expertise and learning. And one is able to eventually reach out with enjoyment to new experiences. How long does this take? It takes as long as it takes. One woman thought it might never happen again. It took years. But it did happen. The important thing is to take your needs seriously and meet them, giving yourself the time and space to heal. Make new beginnings carefully and in small doses. Treat yourself with care, love, and respect. Go at your own pace.

FINDING OUT WHERE GOD IS IN ALL THIS

The reason such conflicts and victimizations cause a crisis of faith has to do with connections in our experience, and thus in our minds, between what we believe about God and the people we associate with who share that belief. It has to do, again, with the *family* of faith. When we are uncertain about our place in that family, we experience uncertainty about God's place in it and the things we thought we knew about him that we learned within that family of faith.

In order to deal with God we need to separate him (in our consciousness and then in our experience) from the people we have associated him with. God is not the Church. God is not the organization. God is not even the people we have loved, trusted, admired, and respected, the people who taught us about God in the first place. God is only God, he is no one else. Would you make assumptions about someone because of what people who claimed to be his friends did? No. That would not be either fair or reasonable. But we do that. Not because it makes sense, but because of how we feel. It is because of associations.

We must also begin to separate truth from experience. What happened merely happened. God is. We may not know God as well as we thought, trusting other people to define him for us. But we can know him. We can go to him in sincerity and tell him that we aren't sure of anything anymore. And we do not even know that we know who he is. But we, bleeding and battered, want to know. And he will reteach us, or he will re-remind us of what we knew before we allowed other people to superimpose their images between ourselves and God. This too may take time.

It will help to deal with absolutes with an eye to determining what they are relative to what we feel. And relative to what has happened, or will happen, or is likely to happen. When you are hurting, each incident or feeling *seems* at the time to be everything—or to be nothing. Take time and search for the absolutes. Then you will be able gradually to see in perspective again, a new perspective, to which you will need to become accustomed, a perspective to which you eventually *can* become comfortably accustomed.

FINDING YOUR WAY

Being cast out of the pseudo-family, losing our position in the family-feeling group, makes us feel very alone. But it does something good too. It makes us focus on ourselves. And that is something people who are submerged in a church or organization learn not to do. We are taught that being self-oriented is selfish, that we should be other-oriented, *family*-oriented. The truth is that that makes us much more controllable. Coercive leaders (benevolent and otherwise) have always used such tactics to increase conformity and decrease individuality. Now you are able to break out of that stultifying atmosphere and find your own way of ministry, service, self-actualization, and enjoyment.

I, being Baptist in background, think of ministry always in terms of service, mutual service. I never think, regarding the Church, in terms of authority, office, or ruling. To me, a leader is someone who goes where others want to follow. He or she has no superiority in essence or in position. And I think that my orientation has much to recommend it both biblically and practically.

If I am right, and ministry *is* service, then we do not need anyone human to validate it for us. We do not need an ecclesiastical body to give us a special item of clothing to validate our ministry, or a special service that passes us into a fraternal group, an initiation by ordeal and touch (ordination seems that way to me). If we are led by God and our own inclination to minister, then we do it. The question is *how*, not *if*.

It seems to me that the how of ministry should come from the same two sources that indicate the whether, promptings within from God, and the inclination of our God-given natures. Ministry is an individual thing. It seems strange, when you think of it, that ministry should be standardized into a certain form done in a certain way only in certain places by only certain people. Very strange.

The primacy of individual responsibility of the believer within the basic beliefs of Christianity indicates that we may not give over our choices for ministry to other people. It is our own responsibility, our own ministry. We alone are directly accountable to God for it.

So, after you have been cast out into the world, wounded in the process, had time to mend and distance yourself somewhat, then you can take up the pleasant task of self-discovery, and in that, the generation of your own ministry. What will it be? What is it, even if you aren't at the minute doing it? That is not to say that it can be only one thing. I actually am not too comfortable with the term *ministry,* thinking that Christians are people who have a relationship with God, not people who *do* things *to* other people *for* God. But since ministry does well as a word to describe a certain intent and type of *actions*, I won't fuss when we use it.

I have admired Dwight L. Moody since I first became acquainted with him. (You do feel you know the man after reading about him and reading his words.) My admiration came from more than noticing his totally nonsexist behavior in a sexist era. His naturalness, humanity, lack of pretension, and refusal to become part of the ecclesiastical, hierarchical structure endeared him to me too. I think he is a good model for discovering and doing your own ministry.

In a day when the clergy were the intellectual upper crust, he was an uneducated man who dared to believe that he could serve God by simply doing the obvious to the best of his ability. He noticed that the poor people of Chicago were not present in the rented pews of the clean and starched, moneyed churchgoers. So he started his work among the slums. His ability to reach people by "just talking to them," a startling contrast to the stuffy orations of most preachers of that time, caused people to crowd in to hear him. He never sought ordination, believing it would restrict his ability to reach a wide range of people. He thought he did not need it. And, of course, he didn't.

Moody looked within to see what was in his heart and within the range of his ability. He looked around him to see what was needed. And then he began small with what he could do. He did that well. That was his ministry. That's what I think ministry is. If you find your ministry that way, the restrictions of form and structure will not stop you or shrink your possibilities.

Being self-directing and God-directed frees you from the hierarchy, frees your soul and spirit, and frees your body to relax. You may find, like Moody, that structure-oriented people will come to you and want to cooperate with you for mutual goals. You may choose to work within some of the structure and move outside it for the rest. But you will not be at the mercy of others to define what ministry is for you, or what it can become. You will be free.

PUTTING IT INTO PERSPECTIVE

When hurting women tell me how they feel in their churches I sometimes suggest they stop going, for now. For some strange reason, that is not regarded as an option for most Christians who are accustomed to going regularly to church services. They take in their breath sharply and widen their eyes in surprise. What will happen if they stop?

If they have learned already, they will not lose what they know. If they know God and talk to him now, they will not stop praying. If they care about other people, they will not stop caring. It is a myth that the pastor, by riveting sermons, keeps us on the straight and narrow. If you are being harmed, then stop the damage. Don't go.

The church is a body of people connected to God by faith. Whether or not they all assemble together in a building does not affect that connection. But the way the official practices are affecting many women endangers them. Getting away for as long as you need to is a reasonable response. It may not be the way a good mother would act. But you are not the Church's mother. You are not the church's child either, needing to obey for your safety's sake. You are an equal member within that body of faith, and responsible for your own self. Do what is best for you. It will ultimately be what is best for the Church as well. For as long as we allow it to harm us, it will. Leaving is a way of voting, voting for change.

With some space and distance, you will be more able to see what you want to do, need to do, to effect change, to engage in ministry, to join with more compatible peers in mutual support and ministry. You may even decide to go back. But if you do you will do so from choice, not from habit or from fear of doing what you freely choose. You will be stronger for it.

YOU KNOW MORE NOW THAN YOU DID BEFORE

My own painful education at first seemed only to separate me from my naive and uninjured Christian brothers and sisters. They did not comprehend what had happened to me. And I did not want to try to make it clear. That is why I understand so well those letters that begin, "I have no one else to talk to who understands."

The things I had learned did not seem to be worth anything good either. I had learned that trusted administrators could cheat and bully, lie and politick. Well-meaning and foolish women could invent and distort, lie and defame. Throngs of equally foolish Christians could believe and act on information not a single one would make any effort to verify. But, later I knew that what I had learned was valuable, for me, and as information to share in many forms. This is one of them.

Everyone learns from these experiences. It's what you do with it after you mend and heal that makes the difference between it being useless and useful.

YOU CAN USE WHAT YOU HAVE LEARNED TO PROTECT YOURSELF

Never again will I be so inclined to believe that I can confidently make myself vulnerable to people who I do not know are trustworthy. I will not assume they are trustworthy because they hold a certain position, or because they believe something that I do in another area. I will think longer and more carefully before I empty myself unnecessarily. One can do the same good work, slower, more carefully, and without such loss. We are taught to not think of ourselves, and that the battle cannot be won by wise soldiers, only by brave ones. Well, it's not a war. Very few things are really war. We are only trained to think that way.

YOU HAVE FEWER ILLUSIONS

I felt badly about losing my illusions. I am not referring only to illusions about the structure of the Church and some of its pillars. I felt badly about losing all my illusions, about people, whatever the subject matter. But not long ago I was reading something, or heard it on TV or somewhere. It was, "The only way to be disillusioned is to have illusions." Disillusionment has to do with being misinformed, mistaken, ill advised. You wouldn't want to continue that way. It is the sudden landing at the bottom that hurts, not discerning the truth. After you recover from the sudden landing, you will see the value in knowing the truth.

YOU HAVE NEW RESOURCES

There is a certain field of physical body work called Feldenkrais that does remarkable things with bodies that have been handicapped, injured, or misused. The method was devised by Moshe Feldenkrais. He had several mottoes, truisms, principles that he imparted to his students and based his changework on. One of them is, "If you know what you are doing, then you can do something else." I find that Moshe Feldenkrais' principle works in many places other than the physical body. If you know what has happened to you, you can determine what to do differently. Through your disillusionment and realignment with reality, you now know how to help other people in ways you could not before. You can share the truth, and share it in new ways. You are a resource for anyone who does not know what you now know.

The crisis in faith hurts. I hope we can prevent it for future generations of women. But enduring it, we will ultimately be more resourceful than we were before. In a different way, perhaps, but in a needed way. Let us extend our hands to each other for mending and recovery, and then for generating new ways of ministry and personal enhancement.

6. A Message to the Church Hierarchy

I have to ask where are the women prophets in our church today, fulfilling their God-given role? I know where they were in Paul's church. I don't know where they are in ours.

—AL VANDER GRIEND

No one is burned at the stake anymore, but careers and psyches are destroyed as required.

—HANS KÜNG

Many men within the Church hierarchy are uncomfortable with recent efforts to gain equality for women in the Church. To some, it seems like sudden rebellion and not at all the way women should behave. To others, it appears to be a passing and possibly dangerous fancy that will eventually disappear if ignored. A hard-to-understand issue, it is difficult to research and difficult to know what to do about it.

I would like to share with you information that I hope will help you in your efforts to understand the issue and the women promoting it. These are observations from inside, inside the movement and inside the experiences and thoughts of the women involved.

From my vantage point as one of those women I will tell you what is happening and why. I will also give suggestions about how you can begin to make changes if you choose to. And tell you what I think will happen if you do not.

WHAT IS HAPPENING TO WOMEN EVERYWHERE?

It would be easy to dismiss Christian women's insistence on equality within the Church as a mere conforming to secular feminist pressures. But it would be a mistake to do that because it would be a dismissal based on an inaccurate assumption. The reasons Christian women are

HANNAH AND HER SISTERS:
A LOOK AT WOMEN IN THE SCRIPTURES

Tamalyn Kralman

Palm Room, East.
Saturday, SESSION II, 9:00 a.m.

lobbying for change are both simple and complex. Simple because what they really want is human rights, the opportunity to be treated as fully human people. Complex because many influences have converged to bring into prominence the issue at this particular time and in this place. You could probably blame it on democracy and be at least partly right.

Women are only behaving as though they believe in democracy and live in a democratic country. In a democratic society issues continually bubble into public awareness for measuring against the democratic ideal. If you look backward at the history of this country, you can see the upward percolation of issue after issue, measuring practice against the democratic ideal. When a rising issue fully emerges, it becomes an irritant, a subject for conflict until substantial progress has been made to conform practice to the democratic ideal—or until it is forcibly submerged again. But even if submerged for a time, issues rise again and again until democracy finally wins out. Slavery was one such issue, voting rights another.

At this time the issue of women's reality and the conflict between that reality and the democratic ideal is in the public arena. That is one influence.

Another influence that has a direct bearing on the present emergence of what has been called "the Women's Issue" is the education of women. Earlier in this century women worked to gain the vote and wider educational opportunity. Many women subsequently enrolled in colleges and universities, entering professions newly opened to them. But several factors suppressed and deflected the movement toward equality, reducing the amount of professional and degreed women. (For example, World War II and postwar re-integration of military men.)

Now, again, large numbers of women are becoming educated, gaining access to information that causes them to believe they can do what they long to do; that they can discover answers to questions they have long pondered about silently. Many of those questions have to do with the disparity of opportunity between themselves and men. Women are looking for answers, and finding them, they are moving on to action.

Another influence, within the Church, is the emergence in recent years of hermeneutics, the art and science of Bible interpretation. We now have a hermeneutic much superior to that of past generations who loved and studied the Bible. The contemporary prominence of hermeneutics provides ready-at-hand tools for discovering information about the foundations for many restrictive and prohibitive practices concerning women.

So the reason women are restless, becoming more vocal, making requests, insisting on more participation is that they believe in democracy—for them too. It is also because they, at last, have answers to some of their silent questions. And it is because they realize the time has finally come for change to happen.

WHY YOU DIDN'T KNOW ABOUT IT

I know it is tempting to believe that only a few women who are discontent with their own personal lives are using equality for women as an outlet, that this whole thing will go away if you ignore it. And I must say I would not blame some of you for thinking that. Not all of the women who work for equal opportunity do so in ways that encourage cooperation with them. It becomes easy to dismiss what they say because of how they say it.

However, please remember your own peers. I went to a religious college and have rubbed elbows with ministers and church leaders for a long time. There are among them many with abrasive personalities and personal problems. I would never advocate dismissing the Christian message because these people suffer from personal style disadvantages. I'm sure you wouldn't either. So let me encourage you to look beyond the first impression if it was a first impression of dismissal.

Completely aside from the possibility of poor presentation by its advocates, there are other possibilities for why you didn't know the inside story about equality for women in the church.

WOMEN'S CONCERNS ARE INVISIBLE

Women move through life wearing an *invisibility* cloak. Like the Middle Eastern *chador,* which covers a woman from head to toe in plain black cloth, we provide cultural fabric to make women invisible.

I was trying to think of when this invisibility begins, how early in life women aren't to be looked at, things about them not noticed by polite people of both sexes. And I concluded that it must begin in infancy for many, soon thereafter for the rest. Our beliefs about sexuality and vulnerability, modesty and chastity, respect, motherhood, and femaleness combine to create an air of secretiveness about the female body, and then the female experience of living in that body.

It isn't that men make women invisible and don't care about their real lives. It is that in the process of growing up, it just happens. Women talk in hushed tones just out of earshot about "female problems." Girls get menstrual periods. Strange and secretive appliances and supplies are bought to provide "protection," as the ads put it. (I always wondered why we needed protection, and from what.) There is nothing so furtive about the personal effects of males that is unique to their gender. Men do not hide to shave their beards. Nor are athletic supporters sold in plain wrapped packages or disguised from recognition. But, of course, they are not quite the parallel to sanitary napkins (another strange euphemism).

If a woman is ill and unable to come to church or a social engagement, men are often afraid to ask what she is sick *with,* because it is not polite to ask that about women. It might be something female, and thus embarrassing. Why embarrassing? Well, because that's part of the whole system of women's bodies and the lives they lead within those bodies being invisible.

YOU MAY NOT KNOW HOW TO LISTEN

I have often read and heard that men do not listen to what women have to say. Some of what I have read and heard takes men to task for not listening and implies a mean-spirited collusion among men to discount what women-in-general have to say. Although I believe I have witnessed some mean-spiritedness occasionally, I suspect the reason men do not *really listen* to women has much more innocent roots than that. I suspect that the most prevalent reason men do not listen to women is cultural, and process-derived, and not personal or mean-spirited.

I think it is fairly obvious that, in our culture, men are generally in a one-up position in relation to women. That is, men are commonly given the positions of honor, responsibility, and high visibility. With that position of one-up-man-ship comes a certain process for problem solving and taking charge that men learn early in life.

Key to the process men use in carrying out their responsibilities is the determination of the situation at hand. Men routinely and automatically ask themselves the equivalent of, "What's happening?" In order to do this they must translate what is going on, or appears to be going on, into terms they can understand. All people who problem solve must look for common denominators they can understand and cope with based on their own past experiences and understandings. Otherwise quick resolution is impossible.

One of the things required of men in this society, besides solving problems, is doing so without too much shilly-shallying and with dispatch. So a man very naturally scans whatever a woman has to say looking for a core structure, or the central facts. Men search for the *what's happening* so they can deal with whatever needs dealing with directly and quickly, and then move on to other things.

What happens when (because of a lack of common experience between the two of them) what the woman is saying is outside the man's understanding or comprehension? The man, in his efforts to translate by a natural and human process information that he cannot use into information he can use, does what all people in one-up positions tend to do when they are stymied. He says to himself, *"It must be something else."*

When the physician cannot heal or cure the patient he says, "It must be some other disease." Or, "It must be psychological." When the therapist cannot reach and change the suffering client she says, "The client was resistant." Or, "He is clinging to his neurosis." The teacher who has not succeeded in teaching the child sends a report card home at the end of the year that says in effect, or directly, "Your child has failed to learn and must repeat the grade."

All these one-up positioned people are indulging in an extension of the natural assumption that "If I don't understand it, it must be, or mean, or consist of, *something else.*" And that something else is determined by the individual (or group) in the one-up position.

So when a man seems not to be listening, or not to be really hearing or understanding, it is very likely because he is trying to determine what is happening. If he does not, from his own experiential viewpoint, understand what the woman is saying, he is in the process of determining (or has already done so) what something else is *really* happening.

This process causes considerable conflict and muddying of relational waters between men and women. One woman, overworked, lacking money, deprived of companionship and help by her husband's schooling was shocked to hear him respond to her misery by citing her request for a new cupboard. He used his provision of the cupboard to dismiss all her long recitation of longing and need. He said, "Why, you said you would be *happy* if you had a new cupboard!"

Which brings me to another factor in men's not listening, or at least the accusation that they don't. Sometimes men don't listen because they suspect that what they are hearing or about to hear implies action they are not willing to take. That, of course is behind many solemn denials of the fixibility of broken things and just nonworking things about the house. It is axiomatic among women (and observed frequently by the children of the house) that Daddy says it can't be fixed because he doesn't want to fix it. Now, before I offend you here, let me add that women use this one too, but in a different way. They, some of them at least, claim they can't do things desired of them because they have nothing to wear, are nervous, or have a headache. The difference that is appropriate to this issue is that women's use of this technique does not restrict their listening ability. With men it tends to.

The habitual processes that men innocently learn from boyhood work together to allow them to be able to move among women as adults, respect and admire and love them, even learn a great deal from them, and still be ignorant of much that women are trying to tell them. Journalist Bill Moyers gives a good example of his own experience with this phenomenon in the following account.

> Quite spontaneously, one woman in particular arrested the attention of us all as she began to speak quietly but movingly of her own yearnings. She said she aspired not to be free of her roles as wife and mother, which she valued—but to be free of those countless and delicately woven assumptions by which a male-dominated society had laid claim to her right as a human being to enlarge the map of her world.
>
> She knew what it was like, she said, to have intelligence no one gave

you credit for. She knew what it meant to possess talents for which there are few open channels of expression. She despaired at the way society measures women's achievements as exceptions to the rule. And she wondered if men understood that women are seeking to fulfill themselves as individuals, to win their rights, without diminishing the rights of men— that women knew too well the pain of second-class citizenship to wish it on others.

As she spoke I was honestly paying more attention to what she was saying than I was to the speaker herself, until I sat up in my chair impelled by the realization: "Good Lord, that woman is my wife."

... Although she had raised such ideas from time to time in our personal conversations, I suddenly understood that I had never really listened.[5]

WOMEN MAY NOT HAVE TOLD YOU

Because of women's one-down position, they are often hesitant to venture a full and insistent account of their deep concerns. Women will usually try the water gently with a toe before jumping in with wild abandon. They do so from long and memorable experience. Free and open expression often does not pay. They test the waters when feeling particularly brave. And if the waters are cold, most women will go quietly away. The issue will remain submerged—but very much alive.

Often women do not even discuss with each other issues they feel vulnerable about. Women who appear poised, capable, even commanding may be fragile and in need beneath the outward appearance. It is one of the ways we cope in a world that does not allow us the luxury of full disclosure.

But when women feel safe enough to tell their innermost longings and hurts the hidden tumbles out. Often all that is needed is someone who they feel will understand their experience. Because of my books and their subject matter, I have frequently been that person. Typically, those who talk to me are hurting, and feeling terribly alone in their pain. Usually they are capable, hard-working churchwomen torn apart by inner conflict. They love God and their church, but they cannot bear the restrictions and abuse it heaps on them. Usually they have been silent about these stresses after their questions, or requests for more equal treatment for women, were met by rebuff or scorn from their local church hierarchy.

They talk to me because they sense that someone who writes about the issue of equality will understand, perhaps even have some information and encouragement for them. These women are everywhere I go. They are almost certainly present in your church or organization.

Another reason women may not have told you is that they do not know what is wrong. Most women suspect there is something wrong with *them* when they are unhappy at being barred from equal participation and from using their abilities in the Church. Many people have gone to great lengths to help them think that.

I have stopped collecting and filing outrageous and insulting quotes from pulpits, publications, and church marquees that denounce women who want equal participation in the Church. When I first began writing on the subject, I started a file for illustration purposes. But so much has been said and written, and it is all so essentially the same, that I don't bother to clip them anymore. But women listening to and reading those denunciations internalize the message. They suspect that they are in the wrong even when their fine minds, spiritual perception, and the witness of the Scriptures tell them otherwise.

It is no surprise that women think it is true that they are flawed. But I had no idea how deeply this belief runs in women until I began writing my first book, *Woman Be Free*. When word circulated among my acquaintances about what I was writing, I began to receive phone calls from women who knew me or who knew someone who did. The caller would say hesitantly, "I heard that you believe women are equal to men and that the Bible supports it. I don't understand how this can be, but I want to know more. Could I come over and ask you some questions?"

Each time, the same progression took place. It takes about three hours to go through all the biblical evidences and explain the several passages that have been traditionally used to restrict women in the Church and society. As I went on through them I would see the women change before my eyes. At the beginning they were skeptical, but very curious with a restrained intensity—wanting to hope, but afraid to, that what I might say would be true.

Then they would become caught up in the evidences and become more intense, freer about expressing their own opinions and questioning me. At some point each one became transformed, changed. Their faces became radiant, more alive, animated. At the end they all left stronger, taller, more whole people. This change was so striking that I began watching for it as woman after woman asked to talk about the issue. It never failed to happen. Since then other people have told me they have seen the same thing in similar contexts.

Because of a very deep-seated feeling of not-all-rightness, many women *don't know* what is wrong. They don't know well enough to tell you. And if they suspect the truth, they are *afraid* to tell you, afraid of rebuff, disdain, and denouncement.

WHAT YOU CAN DO

Since the world is the way it is and women are the way they are (because of the way the world is), there are bound to be areas in which you lack information. The first step toward knowing what specifically you can do is to gather information. I realize that you may have been conscientiously trying to do this for some time. But I suspect that where you have been going for your information is not necessarily where it is. The reason I say this is that we are all educated to do research in a certain manner, to go to reference works, published journals, experts, for data which we then digest in a prescribed manner and thus become reasonably informed. The problem with this method is that it is too narrow and restrictive. What happens if the best information isn't in these places? And that is what has happened here. Most of the people, the recognized experts in every field, are men. So their information is second-hand at best, conjecture at worst.

The place to go to gather information is to women themselves. This is not as easy as I wish it were. Some women will actually tell you the answers you are seeking. But many women will not. They have been taught to not say (it's safer), to not answer direct questions directly (also safer). Or they find it difficult to express themselves directly and succinctly (especially to men). But keep trying. Eventually you will find out what it is that women want, know, and can provide as resources.

OBSERVE

Look at the women around you in your churches, organizations, and private life as *fully human* persons. Ask yourself if fully human persons would be restricted, channeled, directed, or distorted in any of the ways these women are.

The natural temptation will be to make exceptions, to treat women in such situations as exceptions to something, or to put qualifiers on your statements. Such as, "Mary doesn't get paid as much as I would expect to pay a man, *but* she doesn't have a family to support." Unfortunately, even if Mary had a family to support, she still wouldn't get paid as much as a man. Her superiors would just not think about the fact that she had a family and focus on some other reason to not pay her.

Ask yourself if fully human people should be judged on the basis of their individual contributions rather than be grouped together as a class or treated as exceptions who do not have to be taken seriously as individuals. Look around you at the women with whom you associate and ask yourself if you, a fully human person, would feel discriminated against if you had their restrictions.

LEARN

Rather than limit your reading to news items about feminism and its possible dangers to society and the Church, read responsibly on both sides of the issue. Read books recommended by feminists themselves. Seek to learn why they recommend these books. What do they think about them? Why are the books and/or writers appealing to these women? Ask women questions. And then listen and let them teach you.

This may be embarrassingly harder than you think. Not because you don't want to listen, but because you have been socialized to not listen, or to quickly decide "what the problem is" and move on. You may find yourself looking sincere and saying, "Um hum," as though you agree and understand, but find it hard to concentrate and/or follow when a woman talks about anything of importance or substance. Please be aware, if this happens, that it is a cultural conditioning. You have learned this response and you can learn another one—to really listen.

THINK ABOUT IT

Rather than either quickly dismissing what you hear, observe, and read, or swallowing it and moving on, let it simmer and sit. Sift gently and slowly. Think over the information. Give it time. Neither be too swift to reject or accept. And be wary of the "compromise solution," a particularly maddening technique some Christians use. They say, "Well, both sides are probably a little bit in the wrong." It's a way of side-stepping personal involvement that might cause them inconvenience or discomfort. This kind of comment is akin to the old "She probably asked for it" dismissal of rape—the recognition that something unfortunate happened, but not wanting to believe it was as bad as it really was.

BEGIN WHERE YOU ARE

You do not have to look far for opportunities to make improvements. Begin in your personal relationships. That is both the easiest place to begin and the hardest place. The easiest because it is closest to you and changes can be made quickly. The hardest because our patterns of behavior are firmly established with those closest to us. Changes we make may conflict with some of our other behaviors in the same contexts, and trip us up. But hard as it is, it's still the best place to start. Not only charity should begin at home, justice should begin there too.

Working outward from home and those closest to you, look for changes that can be made in your work place. What is fair and right for a fully human person to experience where you work? Does the pay need to change? How about working conditions and opportunities for work of different kinds? Are you listening equally to the concerns of all employees or participants? Bear in mind that you probably cannot detect subtle discriminations you may perpetuate. You will need to ask. And then really listen instead of argue or defend your previous behavior.

MAKE CHANGES ECOLOGICALLY

People do not hold their views and the resulting practices in isolation from their other views and practices. Belief systems intertwine and intersect with each other. Because of this changes tend to occur in layers rather than in one fell swoop. That is, you may find that you immediately see some changes that could and should be made, but on some of the larger issues feminists are pressing you remain unconvinced. This may make some of your feminist friends very impatient with you. And it may make you think that the changes you immediately see are all that are reasonably needed. However, realize that over time one gradually resorts one's belief systems to adjust to any new light perceived. Therefore, changes will continue to happen within one's own perceptions and more outward changes will result.

One comes to one's beliefs over a period of time. Changing of them also takes place over a period of time. This is actually good. It prevents us from making foolish changes that create victims. So, let me encourage you to continue the process, being alert and open to new and valuable information, and ready to implement it. But also, at the same time, be willing to take the time you need to sort information in areas where doubts remain. I am sure you, if you are honest with yourself, can tell the difference between allowing for ecological change and dragging your feet.

SOME SPECIFIC AREAS FOR CHANGE

LANGUAGE

Does language really make a difference? Sociological studies have proved that it does. The effect of using male terms for generic usage is to either exclude females, or leave them in doubt as to their inclusion. A simple way for you to check your language usage is to read back what you write, using the opposite gender, and see how it affects you (Obviously I am not referring to usage that is by its nature gender specific.) Would you, as a male, feel excluded if you heard the sermon, lesson, or example presented in female terms only? If so, make adjustments. Find words that are genuinely inclusive or make a point of including women and girls when there is any doubt.

ILLUSTRATION

When presenting written or spoken material, select cross-gender illustrations. Balance illustrations with the same qualities presented in a way both males and females can identify with. Avoid entirely, derogatory or joking references to women. I knew, for example, a preacher who always referred to "weak sisters" when he was chiding his congregation about lack of conviction and steadfastness.

BALANCED REPRESENTATION

Governing and advisory boards can be balanced between male and female. That is not to say one must be legalistic about it and insist that if there are ten advisors half must be male and half female. But if there is obvious inequity and imbalance between the representative boards and those they represent, then a balancing is in order. And a word about tokenism—tokens are fine, someone has to be the first one, but they are no substitute for serious and sustained change.

AFFIRMATIVE ACTION

Though it might not be ecological to make many immediate and sweeping changes, one immediate change you can make is to go directly to the women who are wanting change and establish an advisory commission. Ask them what, specifically, they want. Meet with them regularly, and use them as serious advisors. Establish a female watchdog committee to monitor publications and presentations, services, and programs for inequities and to suggest remedies. Even though some suggestions may be beyond your present comfort level, make sincere effort to find ways, working with your committee, that you can both get what you want. Set up time frames for changes that need to be made gradually.

One of the most valuable uses this committee can be put to is looking for exclusions and omissions, places where women and their life experience are treated as nonexistent or invisible. It would be impossible for you to detect all of these omissions alone.

WHAT WILL HAPPEN IF YOU DO NOTHING?

I know that the temptation for some in positions of power and leadership will be to read a bit, think a bit, and then do nothing to make any changes. Many, if not most of you, are overworked and over-stressed a large part of the time. You do not need another confusing issue to deal with. Others may be unwilling to make changes because it is inconvenient or dangerous for them to oppose the wishes of people above them in the hierarchy or below them in the supporting constituency. And I know there will be people who remain unconvinced that change is needed or wise.

I personally believe that you should have the right to do nothing, to refuse to deal with the issue, even to oppose equal participation for women in the Church. I do not see how we can have a free and vital Church and refuse you that option. Because I have been involved in the issue for some time and have had contact with many people both in and out of the movement, I can offer you some information about what will probably happen if you do choose to do nothing about this issue. I hope my information will be helpful to you whatever you choose.

CHANGE MAY HAPPEN IN YOUR AREA ANYWAY

The possibility of this issue quietly dying out or slowly fading away is small. Not because of the rightness of the aims and not because of the expertise of those working for change, but because of the historical timing of the issue. It would be wonderful if rightness were enough for changes to occur in any time and place. But we all know that that is not so. And women are no more capable by nature than men are. In fact, women are at a definite disadvantage when it comes to chan-gemaking because of the way they are trained from childhood. But the timing of this issue in the onward outworking of the democratic process and the rise of hermeneutics at a time when women are able as never before to gain educational tools to find their own answers and present them to the world combine to ensure that this issue will endure.

The likelihood that someone else will implement the needed changes in your organization or church is great. And if that happens you may be placed in a disadvantageous position. Unfortunately, issues and personalities easily become connected in people's minds. When that happens opposition to one is seen as opposition to both.

Eventually changes may come about from forces outside your organization or church. It may be that legal or organizational requirements will necessitate a few changes, which will then lead to others. If this happens over your objections, it may be both uncomfortable and disadvantageous for you.

INDIVIDUAL WOMEN WILL SUFFER

Whenever women have gifts that are prohibited and resources that are unused and unwanted, the holders of the gifts suffer. Some of my most earnest conversants have been the sons of such women. I stood outside the Wheaton College campus building where I had just lectured, listening late into the evening to a young seminary student pour out his anguish at the treatment his gifted mother had received. She had been a missionary with a rich and successful ministry. When the family returned to the United States, she took an adult class in their home church, with only a handful of members, and built it into a large and successful Bible study. At some point the church elders and pastor decided it was not proper for a woman to teach adult males and took her class from her. The woman was devastated, wondering if what she had done so well all the years of her ministry was indeed wrong. The son, relieved to have someone to tell this to, was horrified at what all this had done to his mother, and joyful that he now had new information to give her to encourage her to own her gifts with confidence.

Whenever you restrict the ministry of women, you quench the Spirit of God who would have spoken through them. That is a serious choice to make, both because of what it does to the women and what it denies the body of Christ, the Church.

BOTH WOMEN AND MEN WILL LEAVE YOUR CHURCH OR ORGANIZATION

I live in an area rich with churches, especially rich in Christian Reformed churches. And I watch as congregations adamantly opposed to the ministry of women spin off some of the best and brightest to other congregations, and ultimately many to other denominations. The women who leave cannot bear the oppression of silence and disuse forced upon them. Church becomes a place of pain and misery instead of a place of solace and nourishment. They must leave to survive.

Sexist practices cost organizations in the same manner. Though I am sure those in authority positions often do not know the real reasons many qualified and good workers leave. Just last week a capable and experienced woman told me she was looking for another job because of the unremitting sexism of her boss. He probably does not know he is behaving in a sexist manner. One of the objections to his leadership is that she cannot tell him anything he finds uncomfortable. Thus she cannot even make requests for change. He will never know why she left.

Another case that I know of presently is in a parachurch organization. An executive, who I think would certainly not suspect that he was at all discriminatory, is deeply resented by the female workers under him because he takes the suggestions, information, work, and decisions of male workers more seriously than those of the female workers. The discrimination is sometimes subtle, but it is almost always there.

YOUR MINISTRY WILL BE IMPOVERISHED

Not only do men and women leave sexist and repressive atmospheres, taking their gifts and resources with them, but the omission of the ministry of women impoverishes any church or organization in which they cannot fully contribute.

YOU MAY BECOME A TARGET FOR UNSKILLFUL, IRRITATING, AND DISRUPTIVE CHANGEMAKERS

Groups wanting to make changes, of whatever kind, tend to have among them people of varying ability and wisdom. Those who have more zeal than discernment tend to cause problems for both their own co-workers and those they hope to influence. I have personally been victimized by such unskillful changemakers. The women who wanted to secure an endorsement of their anti-ERA activities from Moody Bible Institute did not succeed in their efforts. But they did manage to defame and discredit a valued and loved teacher there and ultimately cost him his job. They succeeded in causing his family trouble and displacement. They succeeded in prompting the Institute to make decisions and take actions that caused it to appear shameful and dishonest to many of its employees and alumni. They accomplished all this by foolish and unethical changemaking tactics.

I want to warn you that all the foolish and unskilled people are not on the other side of this issue. Feminists are capable of unwise choices and actions too. By refusing to take the issue of equality for women in the Church seriously you may attract the interest of some of my not-so-skillful sisters. And they may cause you inconvenience or worse.

CHANGE MAY NOT HAPPEN IN YOUR AREA DURING YOUR SERVICE

It is possible that you may be able to maintain the discriminatory practices of your church or organization during your whole tenure there. And it will happen in some places because change progresses unevenly, lagging far behind in some places, racing quickly ahead in others. If that does happen for you, then you will have nothing to deal with at all. You can continue on as you are now. You will find around you people who agree with you. If there are those who do not, they will leave. I do not know how such a situation can be predicted. But I know, historically, that this pattern does occur in times of change.

BEING BIG ENOUGH TO GROW

I come from a rather fundamentalist background. One of the things I have noticed about that background is the irony of a common belief about change. Among the people with whom I lived and worshipped and studied for many years, the belief was almost universal that rigidity is strength. I listened to many sermons against compromise. Compromise was a dirty word. I think most children in those churches must grow up thinking that. Many of the people I knew and loved thought that flexibility was weakness.

The irony is that the opposite is true, *in*flexibility is weakness, *flexibility* is a component of strength. The inflexible position is brittle. Flexibility means being able to see the broad picture. It means finding many ways to get what you want. It means being able to find ways that two people, or two groups, or many people, can all get what they want without anyone being the loser.

I believe that flexibility is a component of maturity too. As the mother of four, all of whom went through the normal inflexibility of early childhood, with a brief return to that state during adolescence, I have observed the effect maturity has on inflexibility. The flexibility of true maturity can see how the world looks to someone with a different set of experiences. It can search for alternative ways to organize, to administer, to minister, to allow generative processes to take place.

WHAT YOU WILL GAIN

Men who have become convinced that women are fully human and should be allowed all opportunities that implies often say it has been a personally freeing experience. They testify to feeling relieved to no longer be responsible for all important decisions. They talk about how their relationships with women have been enriched.

You will have a more vital ministry. Restricting any group arbitrarily on the basis of skin color, economic status, or gender has a deadening effect. It stifles the freedom and vitality of the living organism that the Church is, making it impossible for mutual edification to work freely through the Holy Spirit. When those restrictions are lifted a generating freedom is loosed. The abilities and contributions previously unused have a proliferating effect that goes beyond their own boundaries.

Because of the increasingly insistent evidences modern hermeneutics has uncovered, an added gain will be a more biblical ministry. Many Bible believers have, for a long time, believed that to be true to the Scriptures one had to restrict women's participation. Increasingly, that belief is falling before superior hermeneutics. Everyone who takes the Bible seriously has a responsibility to fully study hermeneutical evidence pertinent to the issue.

I believe an added benefit of allowing women equal participation, enabling the changes to come about that will open all doors in the church to them, is a deep and rewarding satisfaction. There is something about doing what you know is right that satisfies. I have felt it, and so have you. I think you will feel that when you make the changes necessary to implement full participation, full humanity and its benefits, for the women in your life and in your organization.

IS IT ALL ROSES THEN?

No, it isn't all roses, nor will it be. Change is uneven, and sometimes, like the unpopular part of roses, thorny. During all times of social change (and that is what this is, social change of a most elemental kind) there is uncertainty and unrest. People aren't comfortable with new behaviors. They are clumsy with them. Not only do men not necessarily know exactly how to treat a fully human woman, women don't always know exactly how one should behave either.

Unfortunately, since people live too close to the daily workings and results of change, they tend to think the problems they encounter are caused by the people involved rather than by the process of change that is at work. During the inevitable period of disequilibrium that is a part of any change large doses of tolerance and patience are needed.

There will be opposition to change, and, unfortunately, victimization of people caught in the fault line between opposing forces in the change process. We need to prevent as much victimization as we possibly can, refusing to sacrifice individuals to maintain a certain stance or façade for those who oppose change or who are frightened by it. And if we fail in our efforts to prevent victimization, we must provide support for people who have been victimized, to help them heal and rebuild their lives.

7. Methodologies

When I was a little girl, I used to wish for change, and dream about it. I did not know how to make it happen. Like all children, (who do not understand how things actually work) I believed in magic. Santa Clause and the tooth fairy helped that along. But when I became a woman I put away childish things. Well, not really, not when it came to making change happen. Like most women I still believed that to make change happen, we must be good, stay in our place, and ask someone else to change, or ask them to change things *for* us.

But that only works when (1) You have a someone to ask, (2) the definition of "good" and "in your place" is consistent with who you are and what you want changed, (3) the someone you ask agrees about the change, and (4) that someone can get it for you. And even if all those requirements can be met you are still less well off than you would be if you knew how to get the change for yourself. If you do it yourself, you will be even better at it next time. And there is also all that nice satisfaction you get from doing it yourself.

In the last few years I have been studying changemaking. First I worked at doing it, learning by doing. Then I read about it, learning by research. And at the same time I saw other people doing it, learning by observation. I am still learning about changemaking. A fascinating subject, a whole book or several books could easily be written about the art and science of changemaking.

CHOICES AND INCLINATIONS

Since there are many ways to changemake, you have lots of choices. If you remember the playground experiences of your childhood well, you remember some quite effective changemaking techniques in use there, most of which are, in slightly adapted form, in use among adults now. There was arm twisting, good for immediate compliance if you had superior strength and a quick attack. Social exclusion, "We have formed a club, and you're not in it!" was a good third grade tactic. A stick in the hand and threatening posture would often work; a fist, almost as well, if you were large enough or menacing enough. Then there was, "If you don't do what I want I'll take my ball and go home."

All these tactics, whether used in raw grammar-school form, or more sophisticated institutional form, will work. The trouble is they don't always work as well as we would like. They have unpleasant side effects, some of them having to do with ethics and conscience, others with repercussions. And then, some don't work too well when you are the underdog. And we, as women wanting equality within the Church, are definitely underdogs.

Our inclinations run the range from, "I'm mad as hell and I'm not going to take it anymore," to "Oh, if only . . ." Sometimes we'd like to be nice about it, and sometimes we frankly would rather not be. But, again, inclinations aside, we want to make changes that are ecological, lasting, and satisfying. We want, therefore, to choose the best changemaking techniques and strategies available for our purposes. Such choice is worth our careful consideration.

WHAT I CHOOSE, AND WHY

When I first inadvertently began my changemaking work I had the advantage of having no credentials and no reputation or authority. This meant I could not pull rank on the people I was going to with my message of change possibilities, and I could not use any of the changemaking techniques of the overtly powerful. This gave me a tremendous advantage.

I did not know what I was getting into. For many years I had wanted to write on the subject of women and the Church, the biblical evidences, finding answers to questions I had long wondered about. But I thought I would wait until I had written several books and achieved (I hoped I would) a name with some credibility before tackling what I knew would be an important subject. My projected expertise was still considerably in the future when the women's movement started heating up and church leaders began producing horrendous unsupportable statements about feminist aims. I knew something was needed to refute those wild claims, and needed soon. So I, swallowing hard, began work on *Woman Be Free,* examining those biblical evidences. I thought I would quietly write the book and people would quietly read it, and it would do its work.

Little did I know. My husband said to me, "You realize, don't you, that this will change your life?" And I laughed and said, "I don't think so." But he was right. For the next ten years I was caught up in the movement for equality for women in the church, speaking, writing, answering letters, taking phone calls from women all over the country, receiving visitors from all points who wanted to talk to someone who might understand—and by that time I did.

I did not study changemaking before I attempted it. I learned it by experiencing it, however inadvertently. My advantage from being without credentials and authority was that I had to be thoroughly prepared, leaving no facts half verified, no areas ignored. I also had to rely completely on God's support and presence to go before audiences and sit on forums with people who were credentialed. I had at all times to do my very best. Stressful, but effective.

Working this way also caused me to develop a particular method of changemaking. I could not go before audiences and hit them over the head with my facts. Who was I to do that? I had no stick to carry in my hand, no authority of position behind me. I could not even muster a menacing stance, authoritywise. So I went as a seeker, which I am, sharing my longing after truth and information, sharing the results of my search. I shared discoveries. And I did it kindly, considerately, because I wanted everyone to have all the chances possible to listen to what I had to say. I did not want to close anyone's door to my message. I gave them complete freedom to not listen and not believe, therefore they had nothing to protect themselves from—they were safe *to listen.*

As a result, I was asked to speak in places that were closed to many of my fellow Christian feminists who used a more confrontationalist style. I was considered safe, or at least relatively so. When they needed to allow someone to come and speak on the subject in order to silence the demands of feminists on campus, or in the spirit of fairness, I was often the choice. My point is not that I had a superior grasp on the facts, or that I had a better presentation than confrontational feminists, but that because I left my audience freer to listen, *I had a chance to tell.*

I found that you can say anything, no matter how shocking and iconoclastic, if you use gentle words. You can frame the truth in such a manner that people will take to their books to check it out rather than take to their swords to run you out.

THE PROBLEM WITH CONFRONTATION

I do not want to imply that confrontation is a useless method of changemaking, or inherently bad. It is not. Sometimes confrontation is the very best method, the only one to choose. In such cases I would have no hesitation to use it, and I have. But confrontation is a severely limited method of changemaking. The reason it is so widely used has to do with the form our society takes rather than the relative effectiveness of the method.

We use confrontation because our society is a war-oriented society. That is, from long ago, we have inherited patterns of behavior that flow from the necessity of making war. That is why we prepare young men to be brave, insensitive to their own safety, willing to suffer pain and self-denial, to go against their best interests in favor of group effort for a cause (team sports?). That is why we train a young woman to submit sexually to the strongest and most persuasive man in her life, to define herself as someone who serves and ministers to a man, to consider motherhood a means to fulfill herself as a human being. We want to make sure we provide fighting men, and women who will produce more children for that purpose and support the men who must do the fighting.

Because of this, certain traits are admired and encouraged among us. Confrontation and competition are more highly valued, for instance, than diplomacy and sharing. Our literature, film, art, and folklore all tend toward glorifying confrontationalist changemaking. We also associate confrontation with male-oriented power structures. Thus when women seek equal access to all levels of power and decision making they easily make the mistake of thinking the way to do that is to copy the same methods and behaviors of the people in those positions. It is natural for us to assume that confrontation is a superior method because it is used by those with superior power and who are in superior positions. But that is not necessarily so.

I encourage you to look at confrontation in perspective. We, as women, have access to and practice using some decidedly more advantageous methods, and will do better choosing them over confrontation for most of our changemaking tasks.

CHANGEMAKING CHOICES

Limiting ourselves to a military model for changemaking is to limit ourselves unnecessarily and to fall into an authoritarian limitation as well. Changemaking methods are everywhere; many present themselves from the natural world. How does change happen naturally?

SYSTEMS CHANGE

Changemaking implies a systematic set of situations or behaviors that one wants to disrupt and/or replace with another system. This can be done by changing any part of the system. If one is already a part of the system that needs changing (and one almost always is in some way a part), then one can change the system by merely changing oneself. By doing something different one makes the system dysfunctional. It must change or disband, dissolve.

Another way to change the system is to change any other part of it. This is harder to do, but has the same effect as changing oneself. The system must adjust because the very nature of systems (that they depend upon all their parts) requires that it change in order to survive.

A third way to change a system is to change the ecology of the system from without. This has the eventual effect of changing either parts of the system (necessitating rearrangement) or the system as a whole (destroying or making it obsolete, or perhaps translating it or transplanting it wholesale into another system entirely).

All of the above occur in the natural world. Plants change as their personal ecology changes. A living plant is a systematic entity dependent on many factors, nutritional and otherwise, to survive. A change in the plant's ecology changes the plant because it interferes with or enhances in a particular way the systems of plant growth and survival. The same is of course true for individual animals and animal groups.

The ecological situation in sub-Sahara Africa is in the process of changing people's systems as individuals and as social groups. Those changes are happening in an observable and predictable manner.

SOME COMPONENTS OF SYSTEMATIC CHANGE

When changemaking by systematic disruption one must make sure that one is actually doing something different. It is easy to *think* a change is being made when actually the same thing is only being done in a different way. A case in point is what happened in a church I was a member of. Some of the members had visited a new church some miles away and admired an innovation of theirs consisting of what might be called cell groups within the church. This dividing of the congregation into smaller groupings for mutual support and edification appealed to the visitors. So several people approached the deacon board of our home church, asking if we might do something like it there too.

After several meetings of the committee set up to study the matter and many months of waiting, the dividing of the congregation into subgroupings was announced with much fanfare. More time elapsed before the how and when of the subgroup operation was announced. Finally, the news came through. A deacon proudly told our group that we could send each other birthday cards and call if someone was sick, and send them cards too. A picnic might also be held once a year.

So for all practical purposes, nothing had changed. We were limited to a prescribed set of behaviors that were no different from what had been going on before. The system of isolation and control of all social gatherings by the church hierarchy continued as it had been before. No real change was effected.

People who go to therapists and counselors traditionally fall into the same mistaken assumptions about change. As the late Eric Berne, author of *Games People Play,* is supposed to have said, "People don't go to therapy to learn how to stop playing their games, but to learn how to play them better." In other words, they tenaciously cling to their systems, only thinking (and/or pretending) they are changing.

Women who do not like their own personal systems often make changes in their lives that do not disrupt the systematic behaviors that perpetuate their uncomfortable situations. They are then discouraged when, in spite of their efforts, nothing really seems to be different after all.

In the next chapter, when we look at steps to change, we will focus on determining "What's Happening," which will help us detect the systems behind particular behavior or situations we do not like and do not want continued.

People who get into trouble in a group or organization are often primarily victims of system threat. On a TV talk show Lawrence Peter, the author of the famous book *The Peter Principle* and a more recent book, *Why Things Go Wrong,* said, "Upsetting the system gets people fired, not incompetence." He elaborated that supercompetents and superincompetents are usually the only people fired in an organization. Both upset the system and threaten it, therefore they must be eliminated in order to protect it. Ordinary incompetence is usually tolerated because the system can absorb moderate amounts of incompetence without harm.

When my husband, because of his beliefs about equality for women, was fired from his teaching position at Moody Bible Institute, other factors besides the pressure group from without and misjudgment from within the Institute affected the ultimate outcome. One of the things he did in response to some particularly nasty and illogical bits of business that were done to him was write a letter to his superiors and ask for clarification on and justice in the matter. The letter, unfortunately, was so well written and so complete that it was virtually unanswerable by the organization without upsetting their system. To answer, they would have had to admit some error in judgment or practice, and that was outside their past systematic behavior. (I am not being catty or derogatory here. Like many organizations with almost unlimited power over large numbers of people and vast funds of money, they had developed a method of operation that they did not deviate from. Pronouncements were made from the administrators. Accountability was never demanded of them, however graciously. As my neighbor would say, it just wasn't done.)

By writing the letter asking for explanation, citing the faculty handbook and providing other carefully worded evidence to prove some accounting was needed, my husband put himself in the position of the supercompetent. Since the administration could not answer his letter, and since it was much more convenient for them to not deal with the letters they were receiving from the political pressure group, they fired him.

I suspect that many changemakers find themselves outside their organizations wondering what happened. They have disrupted the system in such a way as to appear as threats to it, sometimes merely through their supercompetence coming to the attention of higher-ups. The suspicion is that the supercompetent will cause trouble eventually by exposing someone else's incompetence, by making changes, by thinking too much, asking too many questions, by changing the system.

So because of what is at stake, changing systems needs to be done carefully. If my husband had not written the letter, the administration could have concluded that he was incompetent in one area and let it go. They claimed that other faculty members were under the impression that he did not agree with his wife about equality for women in the church. (This in spite of many conversations and evidences to the contrary.) Therefore he was merely incompetent as a husband, not being able to control his wayward wife. That would not have threatened the system at work.

An advantage in focusing on systems in order to make changes is that systems change is *process* oriented rather than *personality* oriented. That is, approaching changemaking from a systems perspective takes disagreements and conflict out of the personal realm and puts them into the impersonal. Women, in particular, need the ability to do this. Because of our socialization and our life experiences we tend to focus on the personal. We relate to people one to one, feel personal anger and outrage, and associate bad treatment with specific people who are agents for our abuse rather than associating it with a system of behaviors and situations. As a result, we think in terms of changing people, not ideas, situations, attitudes, and systems. It is much harder to change people one by one than it is to change systems. Also, the people who hurt us often do so out of ignorance and misguidedness. It hurts us just as badly, but the reasons are not always what they seem to be.

If we can approach change systematically and impersonally, then we can remain on cordial, or at least courteous, terms with almost everyone. We will not need an enemy list. We may need a "to be wary of" list because of where certain people fit in the system, and their demonstrated power to effect harm.

Approaching relational conflict and the desire to change the relationship from a systematic position will make change easier there, too. It will also reduce the anger and resentment that tend to accumulate in such relationships.

THE POWER OF FLEXIBILITY

I've mentioned the term *polarization* earlier. I'd like to explain it in more detail and show how it conflicts with a basic changemaking component, flexibility. You will find, if your experience matches mine, that most of the opposition to your efforts to open doors for women in the Church comes from people who have an authoritarian mind set. I find authoritarianism an interesting subject for study. Much can be learned about how to deal with authoritarians by examining their mind set.

They tend to come from rigid parental backgrounds. Early on, they were required to obey strict parents. They always had to determine between two choices: the right way and the wrong way. Since much of the time that is almost impossible for children to do, they were frequently punished. And they were made to feel guilty about doing wrong, failing to do right, and failing to *know* how to make the right choices and do them. They thus feel insecure without rigid structures to tell them where boundaries for behavior are. They will look to an authority figure to tell them "the truth" rather than find it for themselves. They tend to believe there is always a higher authority from which they must extract direction.

But most of all, authoritarians think in black and white. They believe there are clear demarcations between choices. And that is because they think in polarity terms. For example, they give themselves only two choices whenever possible. They will notice one and then determine its opposite. They then decide between the two. If further choice is indicated, they will still tend to choose between two, eliminating one, and then measuring it to another choice. When opposites are not being stacked against each other, attributes of the two choices are taken to logical extremes and mentally arranged in opposing rows to help them decide.

Authoritarians pose many interesting problems in changemaking, but the most consistent one, it seems to me, is their process of polarization. If you tell them you want to do something different, they will immediately look for the opposite to what you are proposing. If you say it will be better this way, they by their own mental processes, are required to discern what will be worse about it—and point that out. One thus *feels* one has to prove one's self to a polarizer. But it cannot be done easily, and perhaps should not be attempted at all.

Because the authoritarian polarizer *has* to look at the other side, it may be more effective to start on the other side and let him or her polarize in your favor. This sometimes works very well and is more comfortable for everyone. But it needs to be done carefully in order to (1) actually get what you want, and (2) avoid manipulating the polarizer.

I will give you an example of how this can work in practice. When I was asked to speak at theological seminaries, I would inevitably be accosted in the question-and-answer period or afterward by a theology student who was going to "set me straight." They often asked a "trap" question or made a statement that amounted to an insult. My first step in reply was almost always to agree with them in some way. I then refused to argue with them by stating that I was only giving an account of my own experience or what I had discovered from my own research. I would then disclaim trying to get them to agree with me, and move on.

This set of steps has the effect on polarizers of forcing them to examine your position in opposition to their own. They are ready to resist. I offer no pressure for them to resist. They are ready to oppose. I agree with them: "I see how you can think that, and it makes a lot of sense. But I wondered, what about . . . ? And so I went looking. And I found . . ." They must polarize their own strong position and look at mine because I have offered them nothing to fight against. But I have not manipulated them or been dishonest about it. I have merely sidestepped their own handicap, and been flexible enough to adjust to their limitations.

You might think of flexibility as having wide peripheral vision in a field of wildflowers. And having only one choice as tunnel vision, only being able to see the dirt path that runs down the middle of the field. Most of the flowers will be missed. If each flower is a potential opportunity, then the flexibility to see and use them all is a tremendous advantage in getting what you want.

We have been taught, and it is kin to the authoritarian position and within the military model of confrontation, that you decide what you want and let nothing deter you until you get it. Bloody but unbowed. I am partly Irish by birth, and I have noticed this trait in my family, in myself, and in Irish history. They fought bravely and well, but sometimes not too wisely. As a result, they lost a lot. Or when they won, success was often too costly. Flexibility might have helped a great deal. Traditional military strategy used to involve marching into battle in formation and firing at each other out in the open. The British even made things easier for their opponents by wearing red—always a clear target. War is an expensive game. But we don't have to play games like that to make changes.

Flexibility means finding new ways to get what we want. Honorable ways, fair ways, not thinking that just because the opposition doesn't do it that way, we can't. Oh yes we can. And it will be to our advantage. The person in any group or relationship with the most flexibility has the advantage. They have an unlimited amount of ways to get what they want. Those without flexibility may have only one.

As Genie Laborde says in *Influencing with Integrity,*

In *Frogs into Princes,* Bandler and Grinder point out that if you have only one choice in responding, you are a robot. If you have two choices, you have a dilemma. If you have three choices, you have flexibility. Five choices are even better. If you are flexible enough, you can correct your behavior to elicit the responses you want. If you have only one set of responses to any one signal, you will not be able to change your behavior when it does not produce the results you want.[6]

So remember as you proceed through the rest of this book and out into the actions you choose that flexibility will be your most valuable asset in making and implementing those choices. We must first know what we want. Then we are almost unlimited in finding ways to get it.

COMMUNICATION IN CHANGEMAKING

Whatever we actually end up doing to effect change, it will always involve at some point communication. We must transmit information to those who do not agree with us. We must educate those who don't know things we want them to know. We have to be able to talk to each other, to work together.

It has always seemed rather funny yet sad to me that every book about family relationships of whatever kind or persuasion always mentions the need to communicate. But they never tell you *how*. They almost all make the assumption that it consists of getting together and talking to each other. Sometimes they will mention, sort of offhandedly, that about 90 percent of communication is nonverbal. And then they let that drop and go on, assuming that no more need be said about this vast submerged iceberg of communication.

It's more than a little frustrating for me to be writing this section knowing that there is so very much to communication that I cannot even adequately scratch the surface here. But I can refer you to a book that will increase your skills tremendously and set you on the road to becoming a great communicator. And I can give you a few tools to help you immediately.

The place to begin if you want to study for yourself and become accomplished in communicating is with the book I quoted from earlier, *Influencing with Integrity,* by Genie Laborde. I have been studying in the area for several years, and Genie Laborde's material is the best I have seen. It works. You will need to read it through, and then go back and practice each piece until it is your own, part of your natural behavior. She writes within the framework of the business world. But the information is easily translatable to any other area of interpersonal communication.

Having pointed you in the direction of expert information, I now want to share several ways you can improve and enhance your personal and changemaking communication skills.

USE YOUR LISTENERS' COMMUNICATION SYSTEMS

The world does not seem the same to everyone. Once I did not know that; maybe (probably) you didn't, either. People process information and store it in their mental storage bins along sensory lines. That is, they remember things by the way they *sensed* them, by smell, touch, inner body feeling, taste, hearing, and sight.

Everybody has a favored system for this work. In the Western world, we tend to favor either sight, sound, or feeling for this purpose. That means that you may, if you are highly visual in your orientation, *see* the world. But the person you are trying to communicate with may be *hearing* the world. If so, it won't be the same experience for both of you.

Listen for words in the speech of your communicants that indicate their sensory preference. Words such as *listen, hear, sounds like, tone, tell,* and *talk* indicate an auditory preference. Such words as *grasp, feel, touch, smooth,* and *get a handle on* indicate a kinesthetic (feeling) orientation. And words such as *imagine, see, looks like, bright, colorful,* and *sparkling* indicate a visual orientation. Then frame what you want to say in their "language."

> We have often found that in family systems individuals are highly specialized in using one representational (sensory) system. . . . Thus in a family system, some members may use primarily visual words, while others may use primarily kinesthetic or auditory words to represent their experience. They are, in essence, speaking different languages. It is the task of the therapist to translate experiences from one representational system to another, so family members can better understand each other. One of the authors worked with a family in which the husband was highly visual and the wife highly kinesthetic. She complained that he never *touched* her when they were in public, and as a consequence, she *felt* like he wasn't proud to be with her. He couldn't understand her response, because people could obviously, *see* that they were together. In order to help him understand his wife's response, the therapist translated her kinesthetic experiences into a

visual one through the following statement. "You realize that when you don't touch Nancy in public, it's like having someone you care about not wanting to be *seen* in your company."[7]

USE YOUR LISTENERS' BODY LANGUAGE

Quite a bit of work has been done in the field of nonverbal communication in the last several years. Books purporting to know what crossed arms means (closed and resistant) have led us to believe that we can tell what people are thinking or feeling by their body positions. That, as has been subsequently discovered, can be misleading. Researchers discovered that women often cross their arms and grasp their forearms not because they are resistant and closed but because they are cold. They found that they could get women to assume that posture by changing the temperature of the room by a certain number of degrees, regardless of the women's emotional state or feelings about other people in the room.

But though you cannot know exactly what someone is feeling and thinking merely by noticing their body postures and positions you can use "body language" to communicate. Studies of successful communication have shown that people who are communicating effectively and comfortably tend to match each other's body postures and breathing rates. It seems to happen automatically when we feel secure and comfortable with someone. If you look around you in a restaurant, you will find people who are pleasantly engaged in animated conversation tend to sit the same and be "in sync" physically. You can use this information to create a climate of optimal communication with your conversation partners.

You might think of matching body postures and breathing rates as a nonverbal way of making the other person comfortable, somewhat like giving them a genuine smile and a comfortable chair to sit in. You are saying nonverbally that you are in harmony with communicating with them.

It is not necessary, or even advisable to precisely match the other person's position and gestures and obviously breathe in sync with his or her every breath. Just casually aim in that direction. Generally assume the same body configuration. You could, for example, match breathing with the movement of your hand or the swing of your crossed leg (moving with the other person's rhythm rather than matching every breath). But don't match directly someone who is in an emotional or physical state you do not want to share. Breathing patterns affect inner states, so if the other person is panic stricken you will begin to feel panicky if you breathe exactly as he or she is doing. In such cases, use a secondary means for matching, such as swinging a leg or hand, or tapping a pencil.

The easiest way to detect another person's breathing pattern is to watch in your peripheral vision the rise and fall of his or her shoulder. Don't be obvious about this. You want to create a hospitable climate, not make people think you are mimicking them. Practice at home and at work with your friends until you can do this technique easily and without conscious effort to maintain it. You will only need to do it consciously at the beginning of a conversation and whenever a feeling of dissonance interrupts the interaction later.

You will find that after establishing a comfortable atmosphere with matching the posture and breathing of your communicant you can then alter his or her posture and pattern of breathing by gradually changing your own. This signals a state of compatibility and harmony that is optimal for communication.

When communicating in a group of people or speaking in public make sure you speak everyone's language by using words from all main systems—visual, auditory, and kinesthetic (feeling). You can match breathing, and thus create rapport, with the person in the group who is key to what you want, or focus on the one or ones most resistant or least friendly. If you decide to match several people, match them one at a time. I first experimented with this technique during a group dinner at a restaurant.

A woman seated on my right seemed slightly hostile to me, the man on my left appeared nervous and tense. While we waited for our food to arrive, I first matched posture and breathing with my hostile companion. When she seemed to become more congenial, I turned slightly in my chair and matched the tense man on my left. Since I didn't want to feel tense myself, and my aim was to help him relax, I gradually slowed my breathing and speech after a few minutes, and he followed me.

I thought both matching efforts had been successful, but I wasn't sure about it until later. As my husband and I discussed the dinner later that evening, he said he had thought it was obvious that the woman next to me was uncomfortable and seemed threatened. But he had noticed that she seemed to change after a while and become quite comfortable. I then told him about my experiment.

CLARIFY VERBAL COMMUNICATION

Verbal communication may be only a part of what we communicate, but it is a particularly important part. The following guidelines[8] can help you cut through verbal communication jungles and roadblocks. Be sure to use these techniques considerately and with integrity. They are meant to improve the quality of information and communication, not stop it altogether between the parties involved.

1. *Ask for missing information.* Look for words and phrases that leave something out, and ask that it be provided. If someone says, "I don't understand," the best-quality information will be obtained by asking, "What don't you understand?" rather than by assuming you can accurately guess. If you guess, you will be supplying information on the basis of *your* experience, not theirs, and are therefore likely to be wrong.

2. *Track down vaguely used verbs.* If someone says, "They rejected me," ask, *"How* did they reject you?" Find out specifics behind the action so you will understand what it consisted of exactly.

3. *Re-form nominalizations.* Nominalizations are words that used to be verbs, but have become nouns. They are passive, wastebasket words that do not help us communicate effectively. To clarify them, change them back into verbs and use them in a question. For example, if someone says, "I don't get any *respect,"* ask, "How would you like to be *respected?"*

4. *Challenge all-inclusive words.* When you hear statements like, "We are *always* excluded, *nobody* could do that, *every* committee member attends," challenge the all-inclusive nature of the statement. Noting exceptions to such statements provides more choices, more flexibility

for being and doing. There is usually a way to get what we want. All-inclusive terms block our way to discovering it.

5. *Question "have-to" statements.* When you hear, "We can't do that, it isn't done, they won't let us," ask, "What stops us? What would happen if we did?" When you hear, "We have to," ask, "What would happen if we didn't?" Again, expanding your thinking past verbal barriers opens new thinking, being, and doing possibilities.

6. *Examine cause-and-effect statements.* Whenever you hear power attributed to other people by cause-and-effect statements such as, "He makes me so angry," or, "They discourage me," ask questions to gather specific information. Ask, *"How* is it possible for him to make you angry? *How* do they discourage you?" People making cause-and-effect statements perceive themselves as having no choice in responding to other people, or situations. Examining those statements reveals choices they do have and helps free them for other possible responses, including no response at all.

7. *Investigate mind reading.* Assuming one knows what others are thinking limits one's perceptions. Investigate such statements as "I know what's best for you," or "I'm sure you haven't considered the consequences." Ask, "How, specifically, do you know what's best for me? How can you be sure we haven't considered the consequences?" Asking how one knows something assumed opens possibilities for a more accurate transfer of information.

8. *Add specifics to generalizations.* When you hear statements like, "It's wrong to disobey Synod," or, "This is the right way to do it," or "That's inappropriate," ask, "It's wrong for *whom* to disobey Synod?" (Maybe we aren't represented by Synod.) "This is the right way for *whom* to do it?" (Maybe it's not the right way for me.) "Inappropriate for *whom?"* (Maybe very appropriate here and now, or for us, or for me.) Adding the limiting specifics to generalizations allows more freedom of choice, more options, and more tolerance—for everyone.

9. *Make sure the message sent is the message received.* Since everyone processes information in his or her own way, we can never safely assume someone is receiving what we send as we intended. If we do not check the received message we will not know. So remember, at all times, that it is your responsibility as the sender to make sure the

message received is the one you meant to be received. *Ask.* And you must ask for *specifics,* not say, "Do you understand?" They may think they do, and be wrong. They may say they do, but be too embarrassed or uncomfortable to admit they do not.

The best way is to ask for their understanding of what you said or wrote. Say, "I want to make sure I was clear in my answer (statement, presentation). Please tell me what you understood me to say."

Then, if adjustment needs to be made, do so diplomatically. Instead of, "No, that's not what I said (or meant) at all!" say, "I'm glad I asked. I see I need to clarify what I said." Then do so and check again. Be aware that many people find it difficult to receive information without reprocessing it. You may be surprised at how many times you must recheck and reclarify with some of them. When I first began doing this myself, I was shocked to discover the extent of miscommunication that had been going on with someone I thought usually understood what I said. You may discover, as I did, that unknown miscommunication has been a major cause of friction between you and certain other people.

8. Changemaking Strategies

Many of us started out thinking justice would prevail and we need do little to help it along. Too many (but not enough) of us have learned that logic, reason, and righteousness are not enough.

Men and women must learn to overcome their own psychological and emotional objections and regard every human being as a real person with talents and skills and with the option of fulfilling his or her creative potential in any way he or she finds meaningful. Women can aid this process—not by arguing but by doing and becoming, for accomplishments bring respect and respect leads to acceptance. Women must now take the initiative. They should seek and willingly accept new positions of authority in synagogue life.

RABBI SALLY PRIESAND

What we are after is religious freedom, not preferential treatment, special favors, or outrageous demands. Because the basic issue is religious freedom, the freedom to worship God freely as we wish, to serve him freely as we are so inclined and called, as freely as anyone of any gender may, our cause goes beyond denominational barriers. It even goes beyond belief differences that separate us from other religious groups. Because of the scope and basic nature of our cause, to attain full religious freedom for women, we can be assured that what we are doing is worth doing, and worth doing well.

To do the job well, we need to gather all the resources we can, share those resources with each other, and lend support and encouragement to each other, regardless of the diversity and distinctions between our religious practices. The object of this book is to share resources that have come my way with all the women engaged in wanting and working for religious freedom.

This chapter contains the how-tos, the steps to making change happen that I and other people have discovered. As you read it, translate the information into a form that is most useful for you, relating it to your own life, circumstances, and wants. Be free to adapt and modify, generate new methods, and invent new strategies. Use the information here to further enhance your own rich inner processes.

ARENAS FOR CHANGE

Previously you may have thought only in terms of *getting in,* of becoming an equal part of the established church structure, a part of your own religious hierarchy. I hope that by now you have already begun to think of other possibilities as well. There is more than one arena for changemaking.

WE CAN GET IN WHAT IS ALREADY HERE

To do this we will need to study what *is* here and devise strategies for a long and carefully planned and executed series of projects to change the system enough to admit us.

This is a worthy cause, and I, by offering other options do not mean to downgrade or minimize it. It is important for us to be admitted freely into all levels of religious administration, decision making, and practice.

WE CAN CHANGE WHAT IS ALREADY HERE

Many of us, both male and female, believe there are things in the Church that need changing. This is a recurrent need, periodically necessary to revitalize and rejuvenate the Church. The deadening process of institutionalization must be regularly cut back, cleaned out, and refreshed. We can incorporate our desire to change what is already here with our work to admit women into full-opportunitied status in the Church.

WE CAN CREATE SOMETHING NEW

I remember feeling disappointed when I was a little girl because I thought everything had already been invented. I thought there was nothing left for me to invent. Someone else had already invented electric power and light, refrigerators, automobiles, trains, and airplanes. I was disappointed at being left out. But then, eventually, I realized that we have only just begun to invent. And that there are many more avenues for discovery than mechanical invention.

Just because the Church has limited itself to a certain methodology and manner of operation for nineteen hundred years is no reason to suppose that that is all there is, was, or can be. The Church has been in bondage. It has been in bondage to medieval theology, to political chicanery, to corruption, to decay, to exclusivism—rejecting for possible service whole segments of humanity. We can create ways to minister, to edify, to support and share, to tell, that have not been used since the first century, that have never been used in the Church, that have never been used anywhere yet.

These three arenas for change contain limitless possibilities for getting what we want as individuals, banded together as Christian women, and in partnership with men. You may want to focus your efforts in one arena, or in two or more, or serially. I like the possibilities in working in all at once, using overlap techniques to do several things at the same time. Whatever you choose to do, be aware of the tremendous possibilities your efforts can generate for all believers everywhere.

STEPS TO CHANGE

Here are the six steps you can use to make changes:

1. What's happening?
2. What do I want?
3. How can I get it?
4. Implementation
5. Evaluation
6. Repeat steps 1 through 5.

WHAT'S HAPPENING?

The first mistake in changemaking of any kind is usually to omit the first step and go directly to asking, "What do I want?" But if you focus on what you want without first carefully assessing the situation, you are apt to choose methods of getting what you want that do not take reality into account.

First, look at the big picture. What is happening in the broad scope of the relationship as a whole, the organization as a whole, the denomination, the local church? Look for systems that interfere with what you want, that stand in your way, that may need to be altered, sidestepped, or carefully ignored (being aware of the consequences and making preparation for them).

Next, look at the small picture. What behaviors and situations exist within that larger picture that affect the outcome of getting what you think you want. How do they affect you and your possible efforts?

Finally, look at the individual, personal picture. What is happening in your own life? In the lives of other individuals working with you or who might work with you? What are your personal resources, inclinations, and abilities?

WHAT DO I WANT?

First of all, what do you want in its larger scope? Equality for women in the Church? Admission to the priesthood? Ordination within your denomination? Determine what the largest piece of your goal, aim, and desire consists of.

Next, in the light of what you have discovered about systems in operation within the area for change you have selected, what is an intermediate chunk of change that would be a part of attaining the largest goal of all?

Now, breaking down the "what do I want" segments even smaller, what is the smallest piece that would be a satisfying and complete step in the direction you want to go? That is the place to begin your efforts. Ask yourself some further questions: "Is it possible? If not now, what is possible now?"

HOW CAN I GET IT?

First, visualize the finished result. What would it look like? Let us say that you have determined that your first piece of changemaking will be allowing women to receive the offering at the Sunday morning church services (this might be too large for some places and too small for others). Visualize the congregation sitting as usual, with women walking down the aisles receiving the offering. Notice how they stand, move, are dressed, and the expressions on their faces.

Next, add how it would look to be one of them. How would the congregation look from that vantage point? Then add sound and feeling to the visualization. How would it feel to be sitting there observing this? How would it feel to be doing it? Practice this full-spectrum visualization regularly to become accustomed to the desired activity. It is a form of effective practice that helps you incorporate new behaviors into your life. When the opportunity actually comes, you will be able to step into it as a natural and reasonable part of your activity repertoire. You will also be able to speak of the desired state comfortably and with natural assurance that it is reasonable and will happen. This reduces apprehension in those opposing the change and those who will be experiencing new ways of doing something.

Determine a first step toward your goal. Practice it in your mind in visualization, as above.

Create a state of excellence for the task. What abilities or successes have you had in any other area that could be used here? What have you done well that you are proud of from any other time in your life or in any other place? How did you do that? What personal resources did you use to do it? How can you translate those resources into this framework and utilize them here? When have you been confident and assured? Can you bring that feeling here and now and feel it again? Make a picture of yourself doing the activity you are planning and add that feeling of confidence and assurance to it. Feel that feeling now.

Wear the clothing that seems most suitable and gives you the feeling of confidence, strength, safety, whatever you need, to do the task. Listen to music, before you do it, that creates the mental-physical state you would like. I used to listen to a particular intense, enthusiastic instrumental piece on the car tape player on the way to speaking engagements. When I arrived, I felt confident and relaxed, able to do just about anything with confidence.

You would provide an athlete with all the things her body needed to run the race—food, appropriate clothing, rest, psychological support. Do the same for yourself.

THERE IS NO SUCH THING AS FAILURE

Great inventors do not regard their unsuccessful experiments as failures. They rightly consider them educational experiences. The reason we think in terms of failure when we do not at first get what we set out for is that we have adapted to a deception taught to us as a means of fitting us into a certain educational methodology.

When you evaluate the results of your efforts, bear in mind that you will learn a great deal—maybe the most important thing of all—from the efforts that do not get you what you set out for. So evaluate carefully with that in mind. You may need to try for a smaller piece. Remember that all complex entities are merely simple parts arranged together. They, in turn, consist of even simpler parts. Break down the task into the size that is achievable. Then do the next step.

Be open to changing your course and going for some other item instead. Your evaluation may reveal a better direction, another, superior, more achievable goal in line with your basic aims. Changing your course is always a good idea when you discover a better way to go.

You may find you need assistance. Then obtaining that assistance would be your next task. Evaluate all implementations as you repeat this process through the several steps. Continue to check, by asking "What's happening?" because you want to be aware of changes that take place, some of which you may help create, and take them into account when planning further action. What you want may change as more possibilities come to your attention and more opportunities open up.

INDIVIDUAL CHANGEMAKING

Quite frequently the women who write to me are isolated from others of like persuasion. They think there is so little, or nothing at all, that they can do to change their own situations, or do to change the Church itself. What can one person do?

Actually one person can do a great deal, especially if she remembers that many "one persons" banded together in intent even though separated geographically, can utilize the strength of numbers anyway. So think in terms of many strands in a huge rope. You are one strand, but together with many other individuals you create gigantic strength. If you take your power as an individual seriously you can become part of that strength. Whenever you act alone on a common goal, you are not acting alone, but in concert with a large group with very real power.

WRITE LETTERS

You can write letters to the editors of magazines that publish articles or advertisements that are discriminatory. You can write letters of appreciation to those who publish articles that educate effectively about equality for women. You can request the publication of such articles. Letters to administrators of colleges and seminaries, heads of organizations and denominations asking for information, urging action and investigation are effective. You might think that only one letter won't matter, because you do not actually see and hear the results. But, believe me, letters do count. Letters got my husband fired—even though the people receiving the letters knew they were not based on the truth and were from uninformed people. They worked because those letters represented money.

USE FINANCIAL SUPPORT

You can support financially efforts you want to encourage and withhold it from those you want to discourage. Write to organizations and groups you refuse to support and tell them so, and tell them why. If every reader of this book who did not approve of excluding women from ministry wrote a letter every month to the decision-making board that represents her group or denomination and stated that instead of supporting that group or denomination she is mailing a contribution to support a specific organization working for equality, the effects would be overwhelming. Only a dollar a month to support the group of your new choice would multiply and make its work strong and effective. How many scholarships for women at seminary would $10,-000 a month provide?

AIM FOR DECISION-MAKING POSITIONS

Women believe that opportunities come to them because they are good, or because they deserve them, or because they are lucky. It isn't true most of the time, but we believe it anyway. If you want to be a changemaker, aim for positions of responsibility and particularly of decision making within your church or organization.

One woman told me, "I smiled my way onto several committees in my church so I could be part of the decision-making body." She said she knew that in order to be effective as a lone individual she had to *do* something rather than wait for it to happen. She is an attractive and outgoing person. She used her personality to gain access to the opportunity to help make decisions. Now she helps other women onto those committees. She also influences many small decisions in the direction that will aid her ultimate goal of opening up all levels of participation for women.

Make use of your competence and volunteer for positions that contain some decision-making opportunities. Encourage other women to support, encourage, and suggest capable women in and for such positions. Women are the worker bees in church. Being a worker is good. However, if we want change in policy or structure we have to be in a position to make it happen. Workers can do that if they band together in large-enough numbers. But individuals can do it if they are able to influence policy and practice directly.

FILL A NEED

A few years ago I received a letter from a woman who said that while trying to order one of my books at a religious bookstore she was told that the distributor had advised the bookstore buyer not to stock it. She was shocked and angry to find that books about equality for women were denied readers by the very people who were being paid to distribute and sell them. She wrote to me to let me know what was happening. And then she did something about it. She founded Galatians 3:28 Press.

I met her later at a convention, sitting behind a table laden with many books her company was selling by mail to women all over the country. She was only one person, who saw a need, and set out to fill it.

So was I. I can honestly say no one took me seriously when I began to write. They certainly did not take me seriously in my home church. I was as diplomatic as I knew how to be when asking questions in class and suggesting other options besides traditionalism. But rather than taking my concerns and evidences seriously, I was, I think, considered out of bounds—and maybe dangerous. I found that I could not even acquire a Sunday School class to teach.

After several years of working in the two- and three-year-olds' Sunday School class, I went to the superintendent and asked him for a different assignment. I said I would take any class, any age group, that I was ready for doing something different. He thanked me profusely for volunteering and said he would find something. He never did. I went back and asked again. Same result. This was a large church in a city with many professional people who were regularly transferred to other cities. Openings to teach classes in a church like that occur frequently. None ever occurred for me, in spite of the fact that I had Bible college training, experience as a pastor's wife, and in teaching classes of all ages. Finally, I was asked to substitute, for one Sunday, in the adult Sunday School class I regularly attended. It was a Sunday on a major holiday, during which most people in the church were away visiting relatives.

When I published my first book, the situation remained the same there. I was an invisible person. I did team-teach a class for one quarter with my husband, but only because he insisted I be allowed to when he was asked to do it alone. Even then, snide remarks were made about my participation by the man who was in charge of that department.

I wanted to write, but I had no training. I went to the library and checked out books on writing. I sat down on my $5 chair at my $5 desk with my $5 typewriter from a garage sale, in the basement near the furnace and wrote.

I will never know the extent of the results of my being willing to write about equality for women in the Church. Many people have told me that it was important for them that I did. I have noticed changes in institutions and organizations that I believe my writing has helped make possible. But I will never know the true extent of the effect. And I am only one person.

DISTRIBUTE WHAT OTHERS WRITE

One woman wrote to me,

> The spiritual and emotional maturity among the women here is exception-
> ally primitive. But the elders, surprisingly, are strong and capable men.
> There is a dangerous imbalance in that the male-female models for growing
> Christians are severely out of proportion. And I do regard this as being one
> area I'm called to. . . . My main responsibility here besides Sunday School
> work is the library. So it is there that I have put emphasis on discipleship
> by trying to get people to read and expand their perspectives and interests,
> hoping (and praying) that God will reveal himself in a much larger way
> than many have isolated him to.

Another woman wrote to me about her job in a religious bookstore
where she promotes books that feature full personhood for women.
Others write to say they have invested in several copies of my books
and keep them circulating by loaning them. One woman asked one of
the pastors of her church to read *Woman Be Free*. As a result, the rest
of the male leadership in the church read it too, and changes were made
toward equal participation for women. As she said, "And I haven't had
to say a word!"

You can promote books by calling radio talk shows, sharing information, and mentioning the book it came from. Ask bookstores to
carry books on the issue, and to feature them in a window display or
on a table all their own. Write publishers and thank them for publish-
ing such books and ask them to publish more in the same field with
that orientation. Donate copies to the public library, to church libraries,
to institutions such as jails and hospitals. Write to magazine editors and
suggest they publish excerpts from books you like.

Ask yourself, "How can I discover all the ways I can be a change
agent?" Then observe your surroundings for opportunities.

PERSONAL CHANGEMAKING

In order to change other people, situations, and systems, we must
change ourselves. If we continue as previously, so will everything else.

I know two basic changemaking processes, and a third that is a variation on one of them, that work very well in changing one's self. I offer them here, tried and proven by my own experience, but, except for the variation, not originated with me.

GENERATIVE CHANGE

Generative change comes from the field of Neuro-Linguistic Programming,[9] a new field of learning about how people process information. Because of how people take in and retrieve information, it is much, much easier to change by *doing something else* than by trying to *not do something*. The mental process necessary to *not* do something requires that you *do* it first in your mind (that is the only way you can identify what it is that you are not supposed to do). What happens, then, is that you mentally practice again the very thing you do not want to do. The undesired action is actually reinforced by this process.

So I am not going to give you a way to stop doing something, but to do something. It is really quite easy, once you get the hang of it, to translate things you want to stop doing into something else you do want to do instead. For example, instead of stopping saying critical things, endeavor to say things positively. Instead of stopping smoking, learn to do something *instead* of smoking whenever you get the urge.

Of course, you can use this technique to do something new that isn't a substitution. In fact, that is it's primary use.

The strategy:

1. *Tell yourself what you want.* For example, "I want to feel secure and confident."
2. *Make a mental picture of yourself in such a state.* What would you look like?
3. *Turn the picture into a short movie of yourself being secure and confident.* Mentally run the movie, watching yourself as you move through a situation, or sit quietly beside a lake, whatever the movie is about.
4. *Rerun the movie and add feelings to it.* Notice how you would feel in such a situation, being secure and confident.
5. *Allow yourself to experience that feeling now.*

You can use this strategy with whatever you want to do instead. In the case of saying things positively, imagine a situation in which you will encounter the opportunity to practice this substitution for critical remarks. In the case of smoking, you would need many different satisfying items to substitute for the instant satisfaction that cigarette smoking provides.[10]

Make sure you adjust your substitution, movie, and feeling components until you have supplied all you need in order to do what you wish. You may need to add more resources. If so, go back to Step 1 and add the missing piece. Then repeat the sequence from there. If you have a complex set of tasks to perform, break them down into individual segments that will fit into this format.

This strategy allows you to practice mentally and store neurologically the process necessary to do whatever you want to do *before* you actually do it. In effect, you have already experienced doing it that way —so you can, of course, do it. You now know how, are accomplished at it.

Unconscious generative change is my own innovation on the preceding technique. As you drift off to sleep at night, and as you awaken in the morning, tell yourself what you want. A simple statement, such as, "I want to feel secure and confident," will do it. You simply tell yourself that, nothing more. Do this regularly as you awaken and go to sleep until you feel it isn't necessary anymore. You will know from the results you get and the way you feel.

You can ask yourself for information this way too. For example, you could ask, "What do I need to know about myself to get the things I want?" The process at work here seems to be that as we are in the awakening and going-to-sleep states our unconscious processes are nearer our conscious awareness. You might say that we have intelligence and information that, for convenience sake, we do not bother to be consciously aware of. But we have much knowledge and wisdom within that we can use to help us get what we want for ourselves, from ourselves.

I find it is important to state my wants and requests in a way that feels right to me. So I may rephrase the request several times before I find the one that seems just right.

Another thing you can do with this technique that actually works (though it sounds impossible) is use it to change other people's behavior. You can say to yourself at these times, "I want John to be more considerate," or "I want Mary to be neater," and change the behavior of your close companions. However does that happen? I think that what happens is that *we* change many small behaviors of our own, unconsciously, and begin treating John and Mary in such a way that elicits the behavior we want. We are actually changing our behavior *toward* them. And as a result, they change too. I have noticed this happening in my own use of the technique.

ASKING THE MAGIC QUESTIONS

In her book, *You're in Charge,* Janette Rainwater presents a personal changemaking strategy in the form of questions you ask yourself repeatedly throughout the day. They are

1. What is happening *right now?*
   What am I doing?
   What am I feeling?
   What am I thinking?
   How am I breathing?
2. What do I want for myself in this new moment?
   Do I want to continue the same doing/thinking/feeling/breathing?
   Or, do I want to make some changes?

Asking the magic questions causes the changes to become a reality for you. You will adjust your whole body-mind behavior repeatedly to become what you want to become, to be more fully who you are. This exercise/strategy is pleasant to experience. And again, from my own use of it, I know that it works.

RELATIONAL CHANGEMAKING

Women tend to believe they are responsible for the maintenance and improvement of relationships between themselves and men. They feel the responsibility to "fix" by some extra effort on their part, any relationship that is in trouble. I have realized since I was a teenager, reading advice to wives in the women's magazines of the 1950s, that we take too much responsibility for the success of our relationships.

But, curiously, we also take too little responsibility for changing what we do not like. We *hope* a lot. We hope that if we are good and kind, and work hard and do our part, it will all work out. And because we often marry with fairytale beliefs, we frequently end up with men who give us plenty of opportunity to hope, and hope, and hope.

To change our unsatisfying relationships, we must stop hoping and start doing. Contrary to the sugary advice from many "Christian" books, you will most probably *not* change an unsatisfying relationship by being nice, obedient, docile, and submissive. I know they all have case histories to prove that their formulas work. But they don't tell you what happened next year, or in ten years, or if these stories are even actually *true*. I know some horror story case histories about women who followed that kind of advice.

If you want to change your relationship because it has become uncomfortable, or has been that way for a long time, first ask yourself the question, "what's happening?" How long has this been going on? Can I find a precipitating factor? Do my relatives have similar relationships? Have my mother, grandmothers, aunts, and cousins had similar relationships? If so, you are dealing with a system, possibly like the following:

Marian's* husband was competent at work, incompetent at home. He behaved alternately in childlike, dependent ways, leaving messes, not finishing jobs, generally being undependable and unreliable. Then he would switch gears, becoming cold, overcareful, suspicious, and demanding perfection. He seemed to be caught in his past, never really having grown up, only taking on the personality of a grown, stern taskmaster on occasion. His tone at such times was uncannily similar to a particular relative of his who had oppressed him in his childhood.

One day, Marian, puzzling over her relationship with this maddening man, realized that her father had some of the same traits. Different, yes, but a similar pattern of immature demands and periodic inconsideration for his family. Then she went back a generation, and yes, not one

---

*Not her real name.

but both grandmothers had had the same problems. They had both been married to immature, coercive, self-centered men who did not take responsibility for their own behavior. The women in her family had grown up in the company of men who exhibited many of the same traits. Children of both sexes grew up expecting men to behave in this manner, not realizing that it was not standard male behavior.

Female family members showed traits that fit well with such men. They were tolerant, strong, supportive, nurturant, and long-suffering. They also did *not* consistently require of their men that they be responsible for their own behavior. Immature and inconsiderate behavior was excused by attributing it to early traumas, alcohol, poor childhood training, circumstances, or just bad temper.

Marian decided that the pattern would stop with her generation if she could possibly accomplish it. She set out to hold her husband totally accountable for his behavior, no exceptions. She also stopped trying to change him, realizing that his improvement had long ago become *her* job, not his. She focused on her own personal evolution and enhancement and found ways to make her own self happy that were not dependent on him or his cooperation. She stopped being either his mother or his victim.

At this time they are still together. He has even made some changes since Marian stopped "helping" him change. But whatever happens between them, she knows that she is no longer expendable. The relationship is a two-person responsibility now, no longer hers alone.

If you recognize any similarities between your own experiences and Marian's, I urge you to invest in the book *Women Who Love Too Much: When You Keep Wishing and Hoping He'll Change*, by Robin Norwood. The author explains how uncomfortable relationships happen, how they are addictive, and how to recover from the addiction and learn how to improve yourself—and the relationship. You can combine her good advice with techniques from the following books for even better results.

Leslie Cameron-Bandler, has written a book called *Solutions,* subtitled *Practical and Effective Antidotes for Sexual and Relationship Problems.* But it is really much more. Written for both therapists and laypersons, it lucidly explains both how problems arise in relationships and how to solve them. For you who have wondered how a relationship that was once satisfying could shrivel and die, this book explains the process of falling in and out of love. It also contains explicit instructions on how to effectively evaluate a relationship and revive it, if you choose to.

And the book *Know How,* by Leslie-Cameron-Bandler, David Gordon, and Michael Lebeau contains step-by-step instructions the authors call *formats,* which lead you into new behavior. Besides formats for improving relationships, the authors also include formats for more satisfying parenting, healthful eating, regular exercising, stopping smoking, and more. It's a new and unusual book, but based on solid research on why people do what they do and how to duplicate behavior you see in others and want for yourself.

Information about changing relationships between women and men is easily adapted to other relationships as well. The same basic principles and strategies will work no matter who is relating to whom.

GROUP CHANGEMAKING

How many is a group? I'd say two. That is all it takes to begin group action. In Australia, Rob and Pat Brennan began Mutuality because they wanted equality for women to be a team effort that brings men and women together, not something that pulls them apart. Their brochure reads,

> Groups promoting feminist causes have been active for many years. In recent times, "masculist" groups have appeared. By virtue of their one-sex nature, such groups are limited in their perspective and resources. Efforts inside the Church to analyse questions related to sex roles have largely been stifled by entrenched conservatism and fear of controversy.

> MUTUALITY has been formed to encourage interaction on such issues between Christians—men and women, single and married. Such interaction will lead not only to a wider spread of resources, both personal and theological, that already exist, but will also counter the social divisions that separate men and women in their understanding of each other.

EDUCATIONAL EFFORTS

Women have joined forces to start study groups in local churches, and sponsor classes and series on subjects related to the issue of equality for women in the Church. Forums and panel discussions have been arranged by women and men in institutional settings such as colleges and seminaries.

A colloquium of scholars assembled in Oakbrook, Illinois, in the fall of 1984 to examine the subject of women and the Bible. Papers and discussions from that event have been published in a book, *Women, Authority and the Bible,* by InterVarsity Press. The colloquium was the brain child of one woman, Catherine Kroeger. She and two other associates assembled a committee, planned, and executed the successful colloquium—raising funds, and drawing participants from the United States, Canada, and Europe.

Groups can be formed for a single purpose and event, operate and disband, or they can be formed for long-term effort such as that of the Committee for Women in the Christian Reformed Church, which has been at work for ten years.

NETWORKING—SHARING RESOURCES

The periodical *Daughters of Sarah* serves as an educational newsletter-magazine, a clearinghouse for opportunities and information for Christian feminists. But I think it is particularly useful as a networking vehicle, drawing women of like persuasion together for mutual support. The Evangelical Women's Caucus also serves that purpose well through its newsletter *Update* and its biennial conferences.

INFILTRATION

Not only individuals can infiltrate decision-making positions. Groups can develop candidates for church office, nominate them, and vote in concert to help elect them.

FINANCIAL LEVERAGE

Money is a vehicle both individuals and groups can use with tremendous effectiveness. Money means much more to many institutions than they would be comfortable admitting. It all too often pre-empts ethics and the education and edification of believers. Although we might wish this were not the case, the information is extremely helpful in changemaking activities.

If women band together to withhold financial support from institutions that are discriminatory toward women, and send it instead to equalitarian institutions that enhance women as equal persons, change can come about much faster. But, to be optimally effective, they must *tell* the offending institutions what they are doing and why. And they must tell them repeatedly. Money has leverage. Use it.

ORGANIZATIONAL AND INSTITUTIONAL CHANGEMAKING

When working with organizations and institutions, it is important whenever possible to aim for systematic changes rather than rely on individuals to make changes within the organization at personal cost to themselves. Bravery and courage are admirable, but unfortunately, will not necessarily change the system. After you are fired, demoted, reprimanded, or shifted into a sideways position, the system can still remain intact. For that reason, it is important to carefully ask, "what's happening?" before embarking on changemaking here. Then determine what you want and go about systematic change, small step by small step.

Institutions function in lumbering, usually inefficient ways, oblivious to logic and reasonableness. Thus what seems to make good sense for change will not affect them. They will establish a study group or a committee and maintain it forever, make recommendations, and probably do nothing. Change must usually come in the side door. Think in terms of getting *one* class taught on women's issues, *one* woman accepted in the theology major, *one* woman faculty member in Bible and theology. Then build on what you have, holding your ground already won.

The strategy with institutions and organizations resembles cleaning an impossibly dirty and messy room (more likely a whole house) and not knowing where to begin. Begin with the easiest piece. Clear a small square foot of space and then expand it gradually, keeping that original space clean as you go. It probably could be called the amoeba process, slowly engulfing all opposition.

When working with organizations and institutions, one must dig in for the long haul, be ready to take the time and care to operate carefully and judiciously, to maintain one's gains and work on all fronts, putting away a few dishes, cleaning the floor near the sink, the window over the sink, the sink itself. Eventually enough small changes will have been made that the system will rearrange itself and your work will be done. But until then it's slow piecework all the way.

SOME CHANGEMAKING PROBLEMS TO AVOID

The nice thing about making mistakes is knowing what not to do next time. Even nicer is to notice what someone else is doing or has done wrong—so you can avoid the problem entirely.

- *Too many items at once.* It is a mistake to focus only on one change and believe this will get you everything you want—as the man thought when he said to his wife, "But you said if you had a new cupboard you would be happy." Women who worked for the vote thought that it would bring everything else they wanted. It didn't. Feminists are now in the process of finishing the work begun by early feminists who eventually focused all their energy on obtaining the vote.

  But the opposite is true too—scattering your resources too thinly will also get you less than you want. So avoid taking up more issues at one time than you can work for effectively. Also avoid diluting your message and intent by allowing side issues and pet theories to intrude into your purpose. Separate groups can be formed to changemake on other issues. Then your people can take part, or not, as they are inclined.

- *Incompatible Items.* Ask yourself if what you are putting together really fits. Will it enhance your main purpose or detract from it? Is quality even and sustained throughout your efforts? Do your printed materials affiliate and connect subjects and items that will create confusion or opposition in the minds of people who would otherwise be your supporters?

- *Outcomes not specifically stated.* It is impossible to attain specific outcomes without stating them specifically. Without a specific goal, you are in danger of not being able to detect when you get what you want. You may, in fact, have no direct route toward it at all.

- *Working on pieces that are too large.* Many tasks are impossible to attain in global form. "You can't get there from here." It is impossible to swallow something bigger than you can chew, would be another way to put it. Neither can you maintain your gains if the chunk is too large, even if you are lucky enough to attain them. Ask yourself how many workers you have. What size job can they do comfortably, reasonably, are they willing to do, capable of doing? You don't want to burn out your group.

- *Ignoring the human element.* Incompatible workers, inexperienced workers, conflicted workers, overextended workers, and overexpended workers all make it difficult or impossible to reach a goal. Be wise about your use of human resources.

- *Misperceiving the opposition.* You want to avoid both overestimation and underestimation of the opposition. They may not be as smart and accomplished as you think. Because you want to join them in their privileged position, you may have given them more admirable traits and qualities than they possess. Be aware of the damage they can cause you, and assess their strengths and weaknesses realistically, before dealing with them in any area.

But also realize that they may be fine people who are sincerely doing the best they know how. They may not deserve the motivations you have attributed to them. They may also be uninformed.

- *Ignoring or alienating potential supporters.* Many Eastern Establishment feminists in the forefront of working for ratification of the

Equal Rights Amendment made the mistake of ignoring women from other segments of the population.

Because Middle America women had not been included early in the campaign, they were not available in large enough numbers to make the needed difference later on. Remember, you need all the help you can get—don't burn your bridges.

• *Ignoring risk factors.* A good motto is to not tear down anything you cannot rebuild. A better one is to not tear down anything at all. Take into account what is likely to happen before you launch into an effort motivated by zeal and "what is right." The people who denied my husband his job and hurt his family members in ways that extended for years never intended to hurt us. They just didn't think it was necessary to think about the consequences of their behavior on other people. They thought it was enough to be "right."

Beware of putting your workers in jeopardy. What will what you propose to do cause in the lives of women carrying out the effort. What will it do to their jobs, to their relationships, to their families? Will it overextend these women, emotionally overstress them?

Be extremely careful to consider whether your actions will discredit your organization. One woman I worked with wanted to charge extra for a meeting and create a financial surplus (which we would not tell anyone about) in order to finance further meetings. I asked what would become of the money if no further meetings were forthcoming. She said the money could be split among the workers (she was one), since they had worked for nothing. I refused to agree to this plan, not only because it was outside my own personal ethics, but also because it would immediately discredit the organization itself when it became known.

As a role model, I think the Committee for Women in the Christian Reformed Church does extremely well. They work carefully and present a quality performance in everything they attempt. As a result, they are respected throughout their denomination. When they have something to say, they are immediately credible. That is a tremendous asset to have.

9. The View from Halfway up the Aisle

Years ago when our children were small and we chose to sit at the back of a church we were visiting, my seminary student husband and I witnessed an interesting and enlightening occurrence. The congregation was going to celebrate Communion at that service, we discovered after settling in. In that particular denomination, believers take a small piece of unleavened bread and a small individual cup of grape juice from trays passed down the rows of pews by deacons. When everyone in the congregation has been served, the deacons go to the front of the auditorium and serve the pastor. He then serves them, and they all partake together with the congregation.

The day we visited, there was a slight problem. Because of an unusually large attendance, I suppose, they didn't have quite enough bread for everyone to have some. Since the elements were passed from the front to the back of the building, only a few at the rear were left out and observed what then happened.

A hasty consultation was whispered between the deacons and pastor. They made a decision and went forward with their empty plates, from which they then pretended to take small pieces of bread, hold them in their hands, and solemnly and prayerfully put the imaginary bread in their mouths. They then chewed and swallowed it, all in front of the congregation.

As we had watched them in consultation we wondered how they would handle their lack of bread. We had no idea they would try to fake it. But they did, without a flicker of emotion to betray their ruse. The congregation, none the wiser, left thinking they had been led by participants, not actors.

That experience has always impressed me as representative of some-thing deeper than the amazement we experienced at the time. Not until

I came to the end of this book did I think of its significance for me and for all of us as women in the Church. I was thinking about the title for this chapter and what I intended for it to contain. And I remembered that experience of being at the back, at the end of the aisle and observing the fakery, the pomposity, and the emptiness of the Church hierarchy. I realized that women have been sitting at the back of the church. We have, since we became aware of what has been done to us, what is actually on the plate and who is passing it, been amazed and disillusioned and disappointed.

I then remembered my experience of what it is like to be at the front, to be in the pulpit preaching. Twice I have, with full approval and by invitation of those in authority to invite me, preached to a congregation. Although I have done the equivalent many times (called something else, like "speaking to us"), only twice have I known the experience of standing before a congregation expounding the Word, explaining, feeding the flock with their clear understanding that preaching was what it was.

Once, when my pastor husband was stricken with laryngitis and his voice gave out after the morning service, he asked me to speak (preach) for him at the Sunday evening service. I used an outline I had prepared years before for a class in the Bible College we attended together. The class, Speech, identical in content for women and men, required men to prepare a sermon and the women a "talk." Mine had been on the Proverbs 31 woman.

The other experience of preaching was on a speaking trip to the West Coast, where I was asked to preach at a Sunday morning worship service in Portland, Oregon. Both of those preaching experiences were deeply satisfying and affirming for me, not only because I was a woman doing something that had been forbidden so many of us for so long, but also because the task itself carries a satisfaction all its own.

I realized this morning that though all of us have experienced the back-of-the-church, end-of-the-aisle disillusionment, very few of us have known the all-the-way-up-the-aisle experience of ministering from the pulpit. It is also the symbolic realization of our goal. Though we want to reach the unimpeded opportunity our full personhood requires, that pulpit is the symbol of arriving there.

We now find ourselves on the way. We have left the back, end-of-the-aisle position. We know the bad news. We know the direction we are headed. But we haven't arrived yet. We are halfway up a long processional toward the pulpit.

HOW IT LOOKS TO ME

Once when I was a lowly student in a lowly college (not realizing that either was in that position) an imperious librarian attempted to humiliate me by demanding loudly the sudden retrieval of a book I had checked out—because someone less lowly than me wanted it. She eventually shrilled at me, "Who do you think you are?" a question that has puzzled me ever since. I know what *she* meant, but her thinking was not, to my mind, in sync either with reason or Christianity. Any person is somebody, somebody special. Jesus thought so. And I always loved that and relied upon it.

The reason women want equal opportunity within the Church is that they want to fully experience that "being somebody" that we all are before God. They want earthly practice to conform to heavenly reality. But I cannot claim to be somebody (as the librarian identified somebody) now any more than I could in college. And that's good for the purposes of this book. You can trust what I tell you to be the accounting of an involved observer, nothing more, and absolutely nothing less. For over ten years I have been there among the churches, among the women, seeing the smiles and the tears, getting hit sometimes, escaping sometimes. From the vantage point of experience, study, work, thought, and observation, here is what I see.

WOMEN ARE MAKING PROFOUND DISCOVERIES

Many women don't realize yet that they don't have to *ask* to be let in to full participation in the Church. They are working very hard trying to penetrate iron-clad hierarchies by peaceful and legal means. But more and more of them are discovering they do not need to do so. They are realizing that they can minister, support, meet and decide on projects they want to participate in without going to the trouble of getting the official approval of a hierarchy that excludes them. One woman sat in my living room and smiled with satisfaction as she said, "The officials of my church are meeting this week to decide whether I can minister or not. And I don't even care, because I'm just ignoring what they say and doing it."

Women are discovering abilities and opportunities they only dreamed of before. They are discovering a personal and group renaissance that fills them with joy and vitality. I see it increasingly when women meet together to take part in endeavors they have planned in order to meet their needs, rather than waiting for others to meet them, for them.

A truth vigor and an underdog tenacity are evident in much that is being done. When I wrote my first book I did so with a poster on my wall that said,

> One person with a belief
> is equal to a force of ninety-nine
> who have only interests.

The belief in the rightness of their cause, the desire to share the truth of the Scriptures regarding women, gives women working for equality an edge. It is tactically much harder to oppose an established position —but much easier idealistically, because of this truth vigor and the tenacity of the underdog. Truth has a fine clear ring. The sound accompanies, and urges, and supports us as we move forward.

WOMEN ARE CHANGING THE CHURCH

When I sat on the sofa with the president of Moody Bible Institute in his white shag carpeted office, he said he was concerned about where the work of sharing the biblical evidences for equality for women within the Church might lead. He was afraid of changes that he feared might happen. He said he didn't know what they might be. But he did not seem to think they would be good ones.

It's true that much will change. You cannot alter such an elemental thing as the position in society of half of its members without setting in motion other profound changes as well. And I am sure I could not guess what they will all be. But some I can see happening already, side effects that we did not actually set out to accomplish.

Within the Roman Catholic Church the priesthood is being gradually emptied of its contents. The steadfast refusal of the papacy to allow women ordination has intensified and escalated a lay movement, set in motion by the Vatican II Council, that is opening up priestly ministry to non-ordained Catholics of both genders.

More and more laywomen are joining laymen as "extraordinary" parish ministers, distributing Communion, serving on parish councils, or administering church finances. In short, they are doing many things formerly reserved for ordained, celibate male priests. In some seminaries, Catholic women preparing for lay ministries are as numerous as men studying for the priesthood.

Other parishes have team ministries in which nuns not only teach and counsel but occasionally preach. They also serve in campus ministries and as chaplains to hospitals and prisons.

And, sometimes as a protest against what they perceive to be male domination of the church and to suit their own needs, growing numbers of Catholic women are devising new (and often unauthorized) forms of the Mass.

. . . A move toward giving women more power was recently made in the Archdiocese of San Francisco, where Archbishop John R. Quinn appointed Sister Mary Bridget Flaherty as chancellor—the highest position ever attained by a woman in a major U.S. diocese. A chancellor, traditionally a priest, manages the diocese's day-to-day operations.[11]

A cross-denominational organization headquartered in St. Louis, Missouri trains both men and women for ministry as Stephen Ministers. Laymembers of local churches receive fifty hours of training to enable them to function as peer-counseling ministers. They help the lonely and depressed, new people in town, bereaved, the ill, the divorced, anorexics, people on probation, and those with other problems. Stephen Ministers work in their local churches as an extension of the ministry.

Women who want to participate in the pastoral ministry are finding more and more ways to do so without ordination. In the process, they are changing the structure of the Church. If ministry is something anyone who is capable and caring can do, then ministry itself will change. Rather than the structured option of the official few, it will broaden to encompass the innovations and talents available outside that small group.

Martin Luther did not set out to leave the Roman Catholic Church. He only wanted a few improvements and reforms. But he set in motion profound changes that extended throughout Christendom. Women are somewhat in the same position. We have politely asked to be admitted to equal participation and carefully presented our biblical proofs and reasons. The answer was, "No, go away." So women, like Luther not being able in good conscience to go away, have set out to do what they think is right, producing interesting fallout in the process.

GENERATING NEW AND DIVERSE INNOVATIONS

Most of the places women's efforts are leading are wholesome and solid innovations. Women and men working together have generated yet more. But among the obvious jewels are scattered some strange hybrids and odd combinations. Not everything invented by woman is bounded by reasonableness and orthodoxy. Across my desk come brochures, newsletters, and announcements that elicit strange mixed feelings in me. While I applaud and want to encourage all women's efforts at finding ways to minister and work together, some of the results I avoid like the plague.

Women are as capable of error and heresy as men. Not more so, as some would have you believe, but just as much so. For that reason, one should use discretion in taking part in and becoming a willing candidate for some of the experiments going on, and that will, I am certain, be yet invented. I won't name names, only advise emphatically: Check it out! If it sounds strange and off-the-wall, maybe it is. Maybe it isn't. Everything new sounded strange at some point. But check it out, and find out.

A LONG ROAD AHEAD

As I look toward the pulpit from my vantage point half way up the aisle, I realize we have come a long way already. We now know the issues, and many of the answers to our questions. We are beginning to know who we are, and learning to like what we've discovered about us. But it's still a long way to the front and up the steps to a place behind the pulpit.

Women didn't think it would take seventy years to get the vote. I still can't believe it could take seventy years of hard work by thousands of people for me to be able to have the same right to vote as my brother. Many of them became discouraged waiting for women's suffrage to arrive. Many of us are going to get tired and discouraged waiting for something that should reasonably only take a couple of months, or a couple of years at the most. But that's not the way things work. It does take a long time, because structure is the hardest thing to change.

We will be doing all the things you can do in the pulpit, doing them long and well, before we can all *officially* stand there. The pulpit will be the last bastion of steadfast traditionalists. They will drag their feet, use delaying tactics, and cling with both hands to every piece of furniture along the way. Their fingers will have to be pried off one at a time in some places.

So gear up for a long haul. Take on plenty of water and victuals. Get lots of good books to read. Allow for adequate rest and recreation along the way. We will all need it.

10. Resources

I want this book to serve as a useful toolbox for you. In this chapter you will find directions to lead you to other toolboxes as well. I wish you all the best as you changemake and get what you want, both in your personal life and in the areas beyond.

ORGANIZATIONS

Committee for Women in the Christian Reformed Church, 1610 Cherrywood Lane NE, Grand Rapids, MI 49505

Evangelical Women's Caucus, 1357 Washington St., West Newton, MA 02165

National Assembly of Religious Women, 1307 S. Wabash, Room 206, Chicago, IL 60605

Aquila, support group for Christian feminist men, P.O. Box 55, Newtonville, MA 02138

PUBLICATIONS

Daughters of Sarah, bimonthly newsletter-magazine, 2716 West Cortland, Chicago, IL 60647

Folio, newsletter for Southern Baptist Women in Ministry, Center for Women in Ministry, Inc., 2800 Frankfort Ave., Louisville, KY 40206

Newsletter, bimonthly newsletter for Committee for Women in the Christian Reformed Church, Committee for Women, 1060 Cherrywood Lane N.E., Grand Rapids, MI 49505

Probe, bimonthly publication for National Assembly of Religious Women (NARW), NARW, 1307 S. Wabash, Room 206, Chicago, IL 60605

Update, newsletter for Evangelical Women's Caucus (EWC), EWC, International, 1357 Washington St., West Newton, MA 02165

BOOKS FOR PERSONAL CHANGEMAKING RESOURCES

You're in Charge: A guide to becoming your own therapist, by Janette Rainwater
Los Angeles: Peace Press (Guild of Tutors Press), 1979.
A practical, innovative, and pleasant book that directs the reader toward self-understanding, self-enhancement, and change. Do the exercises that feel right for you, and adapt any that do not, or omit them.

Wishcraft, by Barbara Sher, with Annie Gottlieb New York: Ballantine, 1979
This book will show you how to find your hidden strengths and how to set goals, with timetables for achieving them.

Influencing with Integrity, by Genie Z. Laborde
Palo Alto, CA: Syntony, 1983
This book about communication is one of my favorites. In it you will find instruction on establishing rapport, getting what you want, negotiating, and much more. It is written within a business framework, but is completely useable for personal changemaking.

Solutions: Practical and Effective Antidotes for Sexual and Relationship Problems, by Leslie Cameron-Bandler
San Rafael, CA: Futurepace, 1985
Another communication book, this one is both for therapists and laypeople. Though it is written from the viewpoint of sex and relationship therapy, it contains valuable material for personal change. The Appendix on the Meta-Model is especially valuable (about communication problems, it expands on information in this book). Be sure and send in the card, or write to the address in the back of the book, to receive the free self-concept procedure. It is a powerful and worthwhile personal affirmation.

Know How: Guided Programs for Inventing Your Own Best Future by Leslie Cameron-Bandler, David Gordon, and Michael Lebeau
San Rafael, CA: Futurepace, 1985

This book contains a series of instructional procedures the authors call *Formats*. Formats lead participants into new behaviors. Parenting, Sexual pleasure, relationships, healthful eating, exercise, stopping smoking, and drug and alcohol abuse prevention formats are included. It's an unusual book, based on new research on how behavior is generated and changed.

The Work Stress Connection, by Robert L. Veninga and James P. Spradley
New York: Ballantine, 1981
I was relieved, when I read this book, to finally discover what was wrong with me. My entrance into the changemaking arena, from writing a book that landed me there automatically, caused me considerable stress. I had wondered what was wrong. Clear and easy to understand, the book is based on research material rather than theory.

Freedom from Stress: A Holistic Approach, by Phil Nuernberger
Honesdale, PA: The Himalayan International Institute of Yoga Science and Philosophy, 1981
After I discovered that stress was what was wrong, I set out to find ways to alleviate it. This book contains good material on breathing changes to use in reducing the effects of stress.

Life After Stress, by Martin Shaffer
Chicago: Contemporary Books, 1983
A good all-around manual on stress reduction.

QR The Quieting Reflex, by Charles F. Stroebel
New York: Putnam, 1982
This book contains a particularly good explanation of how stress works and why it affects us as it does. The author's technique is quick (seven seconds) and effective, a self-complete adaptation of biofeedback technology.

The Relaxed Body Book: A High-energy Anti-Tension Program, by the editors of *American Health* Magazine, with Daniel Goleman and Tara Bennett-Goleman, (Garden City: Doubleday, 1986).
I particularly like this pleasant, easy to use book of illustrated

step-by-step instructions for relaxing the body. It also contains
sections on headache, backache, and insomnia, providing remedies
specific to those problems.

Using Your Brain—for a Change, by Richard Bandler
Moab, UT: Real People Press, 1985
New developments in the field of commmunication have spun off
some fast and effective techniques for personal change. This book
contains some of the fastest and most effective of all. You will
find here ways to learn better, change beliefs, motivate yourself,
and take care of unpleasant memories.

Transitions: Making Sense of Life's Changes, by William Bridges
Menlo Park, CA: Addison-Wesley, 1980
I found this book quite helpful when I had to move from my
home because of my husband's loss of his job. The author explains
the three stages of transitions and how to move through them.

RELATIONAL CHANGEMAKING RESOURCES

BOOKS:

*Solutions: Practical and Effective Antidotes for Sexual and Relationship
Problems,* by Leslie Cameron-Bandler
San Rafael, CA: Futurepace, 1985
Written both for therapists and laypeople, it has a section on
evaluating relationships that is particularly useful. Be sure to send
for the self-concept procedure that is offered (free) by the author.
The book contains a mail-in card for it. If that is missing, look
in the back of the book for the offer.

Know How: Guided Programs for Inventing Your Own Best Future, by
Leslie Cameron-Bandler, David Gordon, and Michael Lebeau
San Rafael, CA: Futurepace, 1985
Contains a series of instructional steps that install new behaviors.
It has sections on relationships, called *Loving*, and *Sex*. The mate-
rial is based on research the authors have conducted on how to
transfer behaviors leading to excellence from one person to an-
other.

Women Who Love Too Much: When You Keep Wishing and Hoping He'll Change, by Robin Norwood
New York: Pocket, 1985
This book is worthwhile reading for all women in uncomfortable relationships, even though it is directly about women in relationships with abusive males and drug- or alcohol-abusing males. I recommend it highly. It makes sense of why a woman might marry such a man to begin with. And why she keeps trying to make changes by getting the man to change even though he never does. I particularly appreciated its explanation of the systematic nature of the problem, how it is passed from generation to generation in alcoholic and "dysfunctional" families. But most of all, the book gives specific steps to follow to change the situation, by changing yourself.

Getting Free, by Ginny NiCarthy
Seattle: The Seal Press, 1982
This handbook provides information and advice for women in all abusive relationships, although it focuses on physical abuse and gives little specific advice for the emotional abuse victim.

OTHER PUBLICATIONS

Working Together, bimonthly newsletter
Center for the Prevention of Sexual and Domestic Violence 1914 N. 34th St., Suite 205, Seattle, WA 98103

ORGANIZATIONS

Center for the Prevention of Sexual and Domestic Violence 1914 N. 34th St., Suite 205, Seattle, WA 98103 Telephone: (206) 634-1903
An interreligious educational ministry

CHARACTERISTICS OF ABUSIVE RELATIONSHIPS[12]

Because one of the most limiting components in abusive relationships is denial—by both parties—I am including specific information to help identify such a relationship. If you find yourself here, get help. You can begin by reading *Women Who Love Too Much,* listed in the previous section of this chapter.

1. *Isolation.* The abusive relationship assumes larger and larger amounts of the victim's personal resources. A progressive narrowing of social and extended family activities occurs. Some women are eventually virtually imprisoned by their men.
2. *Monopolization of perception.* The possessiveness of the man, and his demands, eventually cause a focusing on him and the problems the woman has with him that forces her to sift everything through the grid of "How will it affect him?" He systematically frustrates efforts that are not consistent with compliance to his wishes.
3. *Induced debility.* Coercion, both emotional and physical, produces fatigue, discouragement, and exhaustion. Harrassment takes many forms—from inconvenient demands for sex that deny her sleep, to beatings.
4. *Threats.* Implied threats of various kinds and obvious physical threats cultivate anxiety and despair.
5. *Occasional indulgence.* "Happy" intervals provide positive motivation for compliance and hinder adjustment to deprivation. Since there *are* some good times in the marriage, the victim is persuaded to stay longer, to try to improve it, to "understand."
6. *Demonstrating "omnipotence."* Power displays suggest the futility of resistance. Women in abusive relationships consistently feel powerless. They think no matter what they try, they won't be able to succeed without the man's cooperation, aid, or support.
7. *Degradation.* Humiliating situations, embarrassing possibilities, and implied or stated threats make compliance with the man's demands seem less damaging than noncompliance.
8. *Enforcing trivial demands.* Helps develop a habit of compliance. Since the victim does not know exactly what will trigger abuse from the man, she carefully and meticulously tries to do everything "right" to avoid abusive situations. So she is always focusing on him and his wants, rather than her own wants, desires, and inner processes.

INDIVIDUAL AND GROUP CHANGEMAKING RESOURCES

CHANGEMAKING BY WRITING

You can make changes by writing letters to organizations, institutions, and individuals in decision-making positions. A good guidebook for changemaking letters is, *Better Letters,* by Jan Venolia (Berkeley, CA: Ten Speed Press, 1982).

Letters are only one way to changemake by writing. For those of you who want to go beyond letters but don't know quite where to begin, I offer the following books and advice.

First the advice. Since hardly anyone will actually encourage you to write, you must just decide for yourself to go ahead and do it. If you want to write, but don't, you will probably always wish you had at least tried. Next, be nice to yourself about it. Take your time. Be true to yourself and what sounds right to you. But remember that even the best writers get edited a bit. And the best advice of all: the way to write is *rewrite.* In school they taught us to get it right the first time. (Remember all those essay questions.) But they should have taught us to keep trying, until it's right. So when you read your first draft and find that it sounds like garbage, don't toss it out and think you are hopeless. Rewrite it. That means you fix what you can see to fix. And when you can hardly read it for the cross-outs and penciled-in words, retype it. And rewrite it again—until it meets these three tests: (1) it looks right, (2) it sounds right when you read it out loud, and (3) it feels right to you (in your gut).

For other writing advice about things like query letters (*always* query first), markets, and techniques:

- *How to Get Happily Published,* by Judith Appelbaum and Nancy Evans (New York: Plume, 1978)
- *Writing the Modern Magazine Article,* by Max Gunther (Boston: The Writer, 1973)
- *Writing and Selling a Nonfiction Book,* by Max Gunther (Boston: The Writer, 1973)

- *How to Write and Sell Your Personal Experiences,* by Lois Duncan (Cincinnati: Writer's Digest Books, 1979)
- *The Writer's Handbook,* edited by Sylvia Burack (Boston: The Writer, updated regularly—look for current edition)
- *Writer's Market,* published by Writer's Digest Books, a new edition is produced every year. It contains listings of book, magazine, and other markets with addresses, editor's names, and information about what they publish and what they want.

NEGOTIATING RESOURCES

- *Influencing with Integrity,* by Genie Z. Laborde (Palo Alto, CA: Syntony, 1983)
  Don't miss this one. It's written in a form for business use, but very useful everywhere.
- *You Can Negotiate Anything,* by Herb Cohen (New York: Bantam, 1980)
- *Modern Persuasion Strategies: The Hidden Advantage in Selling,* by Donald J. Moine and John H. Herd, (Englewood Cliffs: Prentice Hall, 1984).
  Changemakers frequently find that they need persuasion and sales skills. The methods in this book are based on scientifically proven principles of behavioral psychology.

SPEAKING RESOURCES

- *Make the Most of Your Best,* by Dorothy Sarnoff (New York: Holt, Rinehart & Winston, 1981)
  This book contains a useful method for dealing with speaking anxiety. I like her use of what she calls a *lectern script,* instead of the usual notes.

RESOURCES FOR DETECTING, UNDERSTANDING, AND DEALING WITH SYSTEMS

- *The Three Boxes of Life,* by Richard N. Bolles (Berkeley, CA: Ten Speed Press, 1978)
  Talks about the three boxes of learning, working, and playing (school, job, retirement) that society tries to put everyone in— and how to get out, and do what *you* want to.

- *A Tale Of "O,"* by Rosabeth Moss Kanter, with Barry A. Stein (New York: Harper Colophon, 1980)
  A clever book of text and graphics about being *different* in an organization.
- *Games Mother Never Taught You,* by Betty Lehan Harragan (New York: Warner Books, 1977)
  Many male behaviors in business settings are systematic and derive from "gamesmanship" learned in childhood. This book shows how to deal with hierarchies that have long been the exclusive domain of men.
- *Toward a New Psychology of Women,* by Jean Baker Miller (Boston: Beacon, 1976)
  If you've ever wondered why women sometimes don't fit very well or comfortably in a male-dominated world, read this book.
- *In a Different Voice,* by Carol Gilligan (Cambridge: Harvard University Press, 1982)
  The author believes that psychology has persistently and systematically misunderstood women—their motives, their moral commitments, the course of their psychological growth, and their special view of what is important in life.
- *Women's Reality,* by Anne Wilson Schaef (Minneapolis: Winston, 1981)
  This affirming and encouraging book explains the differences between male and female perceptions of the world, the causes, and the cost.

INFORMATION SOURCES

- *Handbook of Denominations: In the United States,* by Frank S. Mead, Revised by Samuel S. Hill (Nashville: Abingdon, 1985)
  Useful for institutional changemaking, this book gives the history of different denominations, their current membership, number of churches, affiliated schools, addresses of the headquarters of each denomination, etc.
- *Yearbook of American and Canadian Churches 1985,* edited by Constant H. Jaquet, Jr. (Nashville: Abingdon, 1985) published annually.

Another institutional changemaking helper. Lists of names and addresses of denominational headquarters, officers, affiliated schools, and service organizations will help you locate the appropriate people and places for your change work.

• *Women, Authority, and the Bible,* edited by Alvera Mickelsen (Downers Grove: InterVarsity, 1986)

This collection of papers and responses from the Evangelical Colloquium on Women and the Bible is especially valuable for the chapter, "Strategies for Change," by Joan Flikkema. It details methods for changemaking used by the Committee for Women in the Christian Reformed Church.

TRAINING RESOURCES

Stephen Ministries offers a training program for laypersons in pastoral ministry. Write to 1325 Boland, St. Louis, MO 63117. Telephone (314) 645-5511.

Notes

1. A. D. White, *A History of the Warfare of Science with Theology in Christendom* (New York: Dover, 1960), Vol. 2, pp. 150, 151.
2. Richard Bandler, *Using Your Brain—For a Change* (Moab, UT: Real People Press, 1985), p. 34.
3. Bandler, pp. 43, 45.
4. See my book *Heirs Together* (Grand Rapids, MI: Zondervan, 1980), Chapter 7, for more information.
5. Bill Moyers, "Daddy, Don't Be Silly—I'm a Girl!" *McCall's,* June 1972, p. V–14.
6. Genie Z. Laborde, *Influencing with Integrity* (Palo Alto, CA: Syntony, 1983), p. 131.
7. Robert Dilts, *Applications of NLP* (Cupertino, CA: Meta, 1983), p. 24.
8. These guidelines are my adaptations of metamodel distinctions as presented in Appendix I of the book *Solutions,* by Leslie Cameron-Bandler (San Rafael, CA: FuturePace, 1985). "The meta-model is an explicit set of linguistic information gathering tools designed to reconnect a person's language to the experience that is represented by their language" (p. 223).
9. Neuro-Linguistic Programming (NLP) originated with John Grinder and Richard Bandler. They set out to use linguistic techniques to discover how certain excellent communicators achieved success in the field of therapy. Their discoveries about how people store and retrieve information has led to the development of techniques for making changes and modeling excellence in the fields of education, medicine, therapy, and business, among others.
10. For a step-by-step program for stopping smoking, see Chapter 7 of *Know How,* by Leslie Cameron-Bandler. The material there is also useful for stopping any other behavior. For a technique to help stop smoking that treats it as compulsive activity see Chapter 9 of *Using Your Brain—For a Change,* by Richard Bandler.
11. "Women's Role Grows in Catholic Church," *Grand Rapids Press,* 8 June 1985, p. D4. (Copyright © 1985, *Los Angeles Times.*)
12. Diana E. Russell, *Rape in Marriage* (New York: Collier Books, 1982), pp. 282–85.